© Y. Papadimitriou/Dollar Photo Club

Persian Rule over Judea (538–332 BC)

The Persian Empire ruled over the region where God's people lived until their empire began to fall apart. (The Jews were still under the Persians' rule when the prophet Malachi wrote his book around 430 BC.)

From the time of the first return of the exiles to Jerusalem (538 BC) to the time of the prophet Malachi (430 BC), God's people faced various challenges. For example, they faced resistance from some who did not want the city of Jerusalem and its temple rebuilt (see Ezra 4). But God used the prophets Haggai and Zechariah, as well as men such as Zerubbabel and Jeshua, to admonish and encourage God's people. The result was that God's people resumed the work of restoring the city of Jerusalem and its temple (see Ezra 5–6). During this time, some of God's people embraced various sins, such as marrying unbelievers (see Ezra 9). But God led them to confess their sin and repent (Ezra 10).

Even though there was repentance and reform during the time of Ezra, God's people experienced resistance from various people groups after that time (see Nehemiah 1) and, in addition, some of God's people continued to compromise God's Word and thus became guilty of various sins, such as priests teaching falsely (see Malachi 2:6–10), men divorcing their believing wives and then marrying pagan women (see Malachi 2:13–16), and people withholding offerings to God's temple (see Malachi 3:6–15). Nevertheless, God worked through men such as Ezra, Nehemiah, and Malachi to lead many of God's people to repentance, with the result that the city was restored and the temple was rebuilt (see Nehemiah 9–13). During this time, God's people had begun using a language some call "Imperial Aramaic" (a dialect closely related to Hebrew). The use of Aramaic can be seen in the style of language found in the Books of Ezra, Nehemiah, Haggai, Zechariah, Esther, and Malachi.

From the time of Malachi (430 BC) to around 334 BC, God's people experienced relative peace and prosperity under Persian rule, in spite of the challenges and setbacks they faced. However, during the reign of Artaxerxes II (404–358 BC) the Persian Empire began to decline as they faced opposition. By 334 BC, a Greek general named Alexander the Great began his conquests, with the goal of forming a new empire.

Greek Rule over Judea (332–319 BC)

At first, the Persians faced little threat from the Greeks because their city-states were not united. No one city could threaten the mighty Persian king. However, near the end of the Persian Empire, a man by the name of Philip of Macedon, who so greatly admired Greek culture that he wished to influence other cultures accordingly, united many of the Greek city-states. Philip set the stage for his son Alexander to become one of the greatest military conquerors in history.

When Alexander was thirteen years old, the great philosopher Aristotle became his instructor. From him, Alexander learned about Greek art and literature. Alexander also studied Greek religion, culture, and civilization. During his conquests, Alexander would promote what became known as "Hellenism"; that is, the influence of Greek language and culture upon the various people groups within his expanding empire.

When Alexander was still quite young, he inherited his father's throne and began his military conquests in Greece, forcing various city-states to submit to his desire to reign over a united Greece. In 334 BC, Alexander left Greece with his army and traveled to Asia with the dream of making

The Empire of Alexander

Territory controlled by Alexander

himself ruler of the Persian Empire—a dream he would come to realize in only a few years. After visiting Troy, Alexander moved on to conquer the Persian rulers of Asia Minor. Next, he conquered the Ionian cities of Asia Minor. By the end of 334 BC, he had conquered the cities of Ephesus, Miletus, and Halicarnassus. In October of 333 BC, Alexander even defeated the huge Persian army led by Darius II. After this great victory, Alexander began his conquest of the eastern coast of the Mediterranean. In 332 BC, he conquered Tyre and Gaza, and then he moved south to Jerusalem.

Even though Alexander eventually conquered Jerusalem, he became a friend of the Jews and allowed them to practice their religion. However, the Jews felt the impact of Hellenism. Some Jews were influenced by Greek philosophy and culture. Many Jews began to speak Greek, with the result that the Hebrew Scriptures were eventually translated into Greek. This Greek translation of the Hebrew Scriptures came to be known as the Septuagint (LXX), a work that is often quoted in the New Testament Scriptures.

In 323 BC, a time when Alexander the Great had plans to expand his empire even further by conquering south Arabia, Africa, and western Europe, he became ill and died at the young age of 33. Alexander had no heir who was old enough to rule in his place. His unified empire was divided among various rulers: (1) Cassander ruled Macedonia, (2) Lysimachus ruled Syria, (3) Seleucus Nicator ruled Babylonia, and (4) Ptolemy son of Lagus ruled Egypt. This set the stage for the next phase in the history of the Jews.

Ptolemaic Rule over Judea (319–198 BC)

Ptolemy I conquered Egypt in 320 BC. During the same time, Ptolemy I also invaded the city of Jerusalem without resistance. He established the Ptolemaic Empire. Seleucus Nicator became ruler of Babylon in 311 BC, and he established the Seleucid Empire. The Seleucids and the Ptolemies were often allies, allowing Ptolemy and his heirs to rule Judea from 319 to 198 BC. During this time, the Jews experienced peace and the freedom to practice their religion. Many Jews also became

To the Director

This student folder contains nine study leaflets and the enrichment magazine. Remove the center staple and distribute the leaflets as indicated in the leaders guide. This magazine should be distributed at the first session for use throughout the course.

Enrichment Magazine

IN THIS ISSUE . . .

3558 S. Jefferson Ave., St. Louis, MO 63118-3968

1-800-325-3040 • www.cph.org

Written by Thomas R. Eckstein with contributions by Edward A. Engelbrecht

Edited by Edward A. Engelbrecht

COVER: The three archangels with Tobias, by Francesco Botticini. Art Archive, The /Art Archive, The

Graphic design by Christina Ensign

This publication may be available in Braille, in large print, or on cassette tape for the visually impaired. Please allow 8 to 12 weeks for delivery. Write to Lutheran Braille Workers, P.O. Box 5000, Yucaipa, CA 92399; call toll-free 1-800-925-6092; or visit the website: www.LBWinc.org.

Manufactured in the United States of America

1 2 3 4 5 6 7 8 9 10 24 23 22 21 20 19 18 17 16 15

© Omer Hayta/Shutterstock, Inc.

© iStockphoto.com

From Malachi to the Magi

In 539 BC, the Persian Empire conquered the Babylonians. In the very next year, God moved King Cyrus to issue a decree that allowed God's people to return to their homeland and to rebuild the temple in Jerusalem (Ezra 1:1–4). The Books of Ezra and Nehemiah record events that took place from the time when the first exiles returned from Babylon to Jerusalem (in 538 BC) to the time when the prophet Malachi proclaimed God's Word to His people who had once again strayed from Him into sin and rebellion against His Word (around 430 BC).

Amazingly, the Book of Malachi closes with a prophecy that a new Elijah would appear in the future; but we learn from 1 and 2 Maccabees that no prophet appeared for centuries. Like the silent years when Israel dwelt in Egypt after the death of the patriarchs (c. 1808–1446 BC), the Time between the Testaments had no known prophets. Nonetheless, Israelites were working, commanders were leading, and priests were praying for a better life for God's people. In this article, you will find an overview of what was happening from the end of the Old Testament to the coming of the Christ (2 BC; see Malachi 3:1; 4:5–6; also Matthew 11:7–14; Mark 1:1–2; and Luke 1:5–17). John the Baptizer was born about six months before Jesus. Luke 2:1–20 records details about the birth of Jesus and the shepherds who visited Him while He was still lying in the manger. Matthew 2:1–12 records details about the Magi who traveled to the area of Jerusalem to worship the "king of the Jews" (see Matthew 2:2). The Magi eventually found Jesus living in a house (see Matthew 2:9–16); this was at least several months after His birth, but He may have been two years old.

© Zvonimir Atletic/Shutterstock, Inc.

residents of Egypt and, while living there, they had freedom to practice their religion. However, during the reign of Ptolemy IV Philopator (221–204 BC), things changed for the Jews. Not only was their religious freedom taken away, but other peoples of the region also often persecuted them. This was especially the case for the Jews living in Egypt during this time.

In 204 BC, Ptolemy V, only an infant at the time, became heir of the throne of his father, Ptolemy IV. The kings of Macedonia and Syria saw this as an opportunity to attack Egypt and her outlying provinces. Antiochus III conquered Jerusalem and also planned to attack Egypt. However, in 198 BC, under pressure from the Romans who were protecting Egypt at the time, Antiochus III instead made a peace treaty, with the result that the Ptolemies gave up the regions of Phoenicia and Judea to the Seleucids in Syria. Thus ended the reign of the Egyptian Ptolemies over Judea.

Seleucid Rule over Judea (198–165 BC)

Judea was under the authority of various Seleucid rulers until 164 BC. After the Battle of Ipsus in 301 BC, Asia Minor and Syria were under the control of Seleucus I—and it is this time period forward that is treated in the history of God's people as recorded in 1 Maccabees.

Antiochus III ruled from 223 to 187 BC, and he began his rule over Judea in 198 BC. At first, Antiochus III showed much favor to the Jews in Judea, giving them freedom to practice their religion and also freedom from taxes. During this same time, many Jews settled in various regions, such as Babylon, Joppa, Galilee, Phrygia, Lydia, Hyrcania, Cyrenaica, and Egypt.

In 190 BC, Antiochus III decided to fight the Romans, who utterly defeated him. As a result, Antiochus III lost much of his territory and was required to pay huge taxes to Rome. In order to pay this tribute to Rome, Antiochus III robbed the Jerusalem temple—and thus began the decline of freedoms and privileges enjoyed by the Jews under the Seleucids. From 187 to 175 BC, Judea was ruled by Seleucus IV Philopater, who was also required to pay taxes to Rome. Like Antiochus III, he also attempted to rob the temple in Jerusalem, but the Jews resisted his efforts and thwarted his plan (1 Maccabees 3:1–40).

Antiochus IV Epiphanes ruled Judea from 175 to 164 BC. His oppression of the Jews in Judea greatly surpassed any Seleucid ruler before him. Antiochus IV was a great promoter of Hellenism, and so he did his best to force the Jews to adopt Greek customs. He even forbad many Jewish laws and rituals, with the punishment of death for those who did not obey. Antiochus IV also desecrated the Jerusalem temple by setting up an altar dedicated to Zeus and then sacrificing pigs there. These events are described in 1 Maccabees 1:44–50:

> *And the king sent letters by messengers to Jerusalem and the cities of Judah; he directed them to follow customs strange to the land, to forbid whole burnt offerings and sacrifice and drink offering in the sanctuary, to profane Sabbaths and feasts, to defile the sanctuary and priests, to build altars and sacred precincts and shrines for idols, to sacrifice swine and unclean animals, and to leave their sons uncircumcised. They were to make themselves abominable by everything unclean and profane, so that they should forget the law and change all the ordinances. "And whoever does not obey the command of the king shall die."*

During this time, many Jews compromised their faith and adopted Greek customs. They strayed from the faith to which the Lord called them and that so many prophets had borne witness against. Some Jews, however, refused to compromise their faith. The resulting persecution—and their example of faithfulness to God's will even to the point of death—inspired many other Jews to take a stand.

The Maccabees (165–134 BC)

The Jewish family that came to be known as the Maccabees began to lead a revolt against Seleucid oppression when Appelles, an officer of Antiochus IV, commanded a Jewish priest by the name of Mattathias to offer a sacrifice to a heathen god. Mattathias refused, and, as recorded in 1 Maccabees 2:21–22, he responded, "Far be it from us to desert the law and the ordinances. We will not obey the king's words by turning aside from our religion to the right hand or to the left." When another Jew who was there volunteered to offer the pagan sacrifice, Mattathias killed him as well as Appelles. This zealous attack began the Jewish revolt against the Seleucids. Mattathias had five sons: John, Simon, Judas, Eleazar, and Jonathan. Before Mattathias died, he appointed his third son, Judas, to lead the revolt in his place. Judas was later given the name "Maccabeus," which likely means "the hammer."

The Hasmonean Conquest

Greatest extent of Hasmonean control

Lutheran Bible Companion, © CPH

Judas and his brothers led the Jews to victory over their Seleucid oppressors. As a result, the Jews in Judea and Jerusalem were under their own rule from 165 to 134 BC—with the exception of brief periods of time when the Seleucids invaded Judea and Jerusalem. Judas Maccabeus ruled from 165 to 161 BC. Jonathan, his brother, then ruled from 160 to 142 BC. Simon ruled from 142 to 134 BC. Simon's murder in 134 BC set the stage for the next phase in history for the Jews under the rule of the Hasmoneans.

The Hasmoneans (134–63 BC)

The name *Hasmoneans* is likely based on the Greek word *Hashmonaios*, which refers to a place-name associated with the priest Mattathias, who began the Maccabean revolt in 167 BC. Mattathias's grandson, John Hyrcanus (son of Simon), began his rule in 134 BC. This was the beginning of the Hasmonean rule over Judea.

John Hyrcanus was able to enlarge his Judean kingdom to the same size as the territory king Solomon ruled in the tenth century BC. Hyrcanus fought against the Samaritans and Idumeans and forced them to submit to Jewish practices—including circumcision. However, there was tension among various groups of the Jews during the reign of Hyrcanus. From this time forward, three separate groups among the Jews were formed:

Pharisees. Jews who, during the Maccabean period, stressed obedience to God's laws and developed a tradition of strict regulations based on their interpretation of the Old Testament—the obedience of which they taught was necessary to win God's favor.

Sadducees. Jews who held to the Law of Moses but rejected various interpretations of that law by the Pharisees, such as the existence of angels and the resurrection of the body. The Sadducees also did not long for a Messiah to the extent that other Jewish groups did.

Essenes. An ascetic group that lived in the wilderness near Jerusalem, Judea, and around the Dead Sea; they considered themselves to be the few Jews who were truly faithful to God's laws, and they dedicated themselves to remain separate from the evil influences of the world.

Hyrcanus's son Judah Aristobulus inherited his father's throne via deceit and murder. Aristobulus ruled Judea from 104 to 103 BC. He promoted Greek culture among the Jews and thus tempted some Jews to compromise their faith. Aristobulus appointed his wife, Alexandra, to succeed him. But after he died, she married his brother Alexander Jannaeus and made him king. From 103 to 76 BC, Alexander Jannaeus also promoted Greek culture among the Jews to the point that the Pharisees resisted his rule and he persecuted them ruthlessly. After his death, his wife, Alexandra, took over his throne, and she ruled Judea from 76 to 67 BC. Alexandra took the side of the Pharisees and instituted various reforms in Judea, thus resisting the influence of Hellenism. Jewish children were educated in the laws of their religion. Alexandra appointed her son and high priest Hyrcanus II to succeed her after her death. But Hyrcanus II had limited success, due to the rebellion of his younger brother Aristobulus II. Civil war broke out in Judea, and eventually the Judeans appealed to Rome to bring about peace. Rome took advantage of the situation and made Judea part of their empire in 63 BC.

The Romans (63 BC–AD 135)

After Rome took over Judea in 63 BC, it appointed Antipater of Idumaea ruler over Judea, and he ruled until his death in 43 BC. After the death of Antipater, Rome appointed a man named Phasael as ruler of Judea and a man named Herod as ruler of Galilee. By 42 BC, Herod was able, by bribery, to convince Rome to appoint Phasael and Herod as joint rulers of Judea. Eventually, around 37 BC, Herod became the sole ruler of Judea—and thus he became known as Herod the Great. This is the same Herod the Great who ruled over Judea when the Magi came to worship the one born "King of the Jews." This same Herod ordered the death of innocent Jewish children in the area of Bethlehem in the hope that he could murder this king whom he considered to be a threat to his own throne.

The civil strife that brought the Romans to Judea and carried Herod to the throne helps us understand Herod's fear of a child born "King of the Jews." Herod was accustomed to rivalry and to winning. So the story of the Savior begins during the reign of this cruel despot, although the story of salvation began long before, when the Lord showed the prophets these days to come.

Thanks be to God! With the advent of Jesus Christ, the prophets began again to speak!

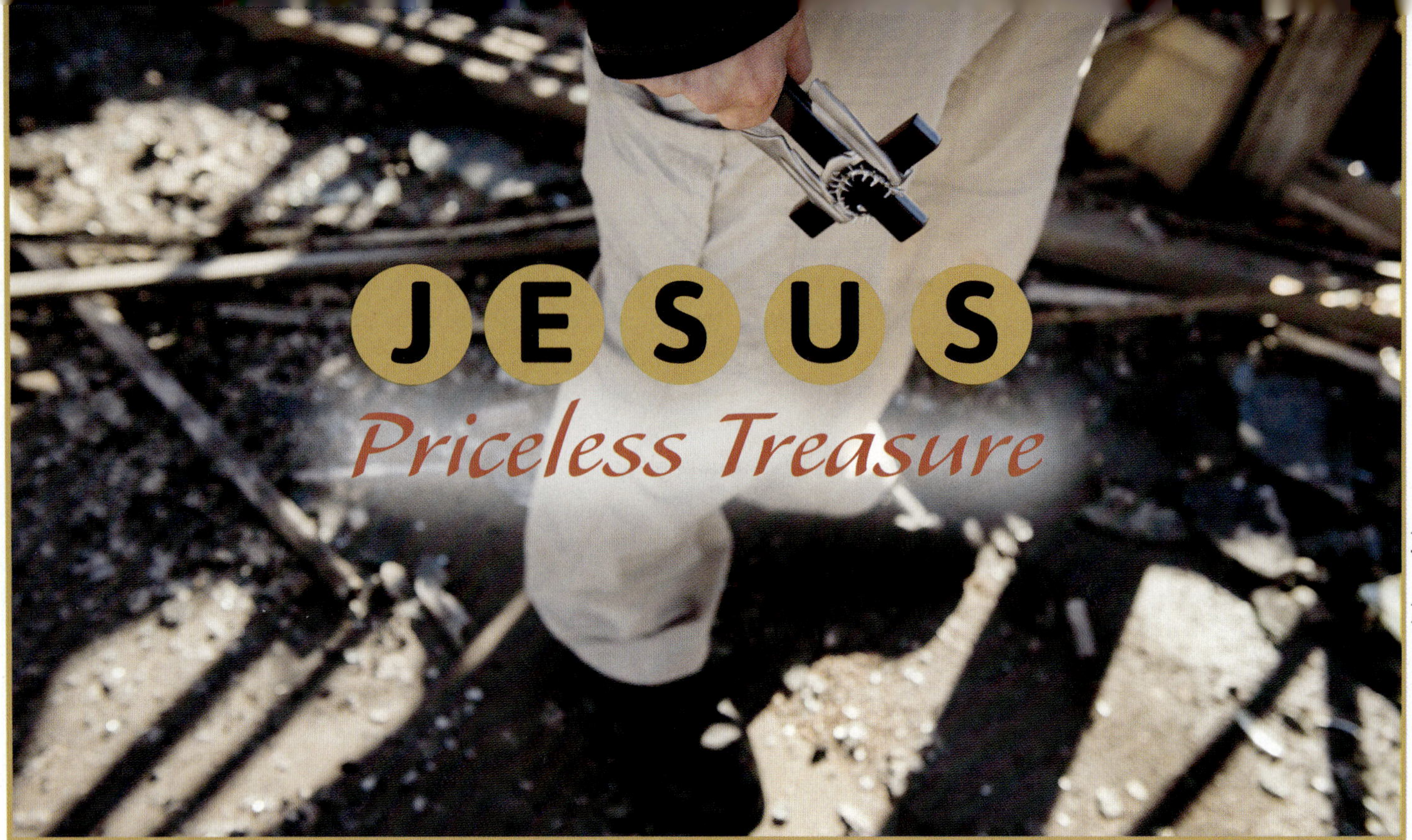

JESUS Priceless Treasure

An LCMS pastor in Ferguson, Missouri/Erik M. Lunsford

In 2014, businessman and investor Warren Buffet donated a record-setting $2.8 billion worth of stock to the Bill and Melinda Gates Foundation, which would in turn use the donation for charitable work around the world. Charities, including churches and faith-based organizations, depend on such generosity to carry out their missions, as they hope to improve our world or prepare people for the world to come.

Yet there are things that neither charity nor any amount of money can do. In this article, we will consider the worth of charity in the eyes of God and its place in the lives of believers today. In other words, we Christians are free to give to others because we know our true treasure is Jesus and the salvation He won for us by His death and resurrection (see Luke 12:22–34; 2 Corinthians 8:7–9; 1 Peter 1:3–9).

Confusing Accounting

One reason the reformer Martin Luther rejected the Apocrypha as part of the canon of Scripture is that it had been used in his day to promote false teaching. For example, Tobit 4:7–11 teaches the idea that the giving of alms—that is, acts of charity to benefit the poor—can actually atone for one's sins and deliver one from death. Tobit 12:9 also states, "For almsgiving delivers from death, and it will purge away every sin. Those who perform deeds of charity and of righteousness will have fullness of life." But the author of Tobit was not the only writer from the Time between the Testaments who had an exalted view of charity. Jesus son of Sirach wrote, "Water will extinguish a blazing fire: and almsgiving will atone for sin" (Ecclesiasticus 3:30).

Certainly, God wants us to help the poor. The Bible is abundantly clear on this point in both the Old and New Testaments. For example, in Galatians 2:10, Paul teaches that one important goal of the apostles was to help the poor. In fact, Paul dedicated much time and energy collecting an offering to help persecuted Christians in Judea (2 Corinthians 8:1–9). We Western Christians must remember that we are rich compared to many who live in other less prosperous nations. The apostle Paul counsels us:

> *As for the rich in this present age, charge them not to be haughty, nor to set their hopes on the uncertainty of riches, but on God, who richly provides us with everything to enjoy. They are to do good, to be rich in good works, to be generous and ready to share, thus storing up treasure for themselves as a good foundation for the future, so that they may take hold of that which is truly life. (1 Timothy 6:17–19)*

When Paul speaks of "storing up treasure … as a good foundation for the future," he does not mean that our gifts to the poor atone for sin or merit eternal life. Instead, Paul means that when the forgiveness and love that God has freely given us move us to give to the poor out of love for God and love for our neighbor, then we know what our treasure really is.

Come, Follow Me

This is what Jesus means when He says the following to a rich man who thought he had earned eternal life by his obedience of God's commandments: "One thing you still lack. Sell all that you have and distribute to the poor, and you will have treasure in heaven; and come, follow Me" (Luke 18:22). Jesus knew that this rich man worshiped his wealth not only because of his greed but also because he thought his wealth was a reward he had received from God because of his obedience to the commandments. This man lacked repentance and faith in Jesus as His Savior. Therefore, Jesus asks this man to forsake his false god (i.e., his wealth) and then give to the poor—the people the rich man thought were poor probably because they had not obeyed God's commandments as well as he had. Finally, Jesus invites this rich man to follow Him. Jesus wants this rich man to see that Jesus is his real treasure. Only when we believe that we are unworthy sinners who are saved by the atoning work of God's Son for us can we begin to give to the poor for the right reasons.

How to Give

Jesus does not want us to give to the poor with the goal of impressing God and men. In Matthew 6:2–4, Jesus teaches we should give without expecting praise from God or men, because God rewards only those who are "poor in spirit" (see Matthew 5:3); that is, repentant sinners whose acts of mercy flow from a heart made new by Christ's act of mercy for us (see Matthew 20:28). We should not perform good works, such as giving to the poor, with the attitude that we are thereby earning God's blessing and placing Him in our debt. Instead, in Luke 17:10 Jesus teaches us that we deserve nothing from God and that serving Him is a privilege.

Our good works are pleasing to God only when they flow from faith in Christ (see Matthew 7:17–18; John 15:5; Romans 12:1–2; Galatians 2:20; Ephesians 2:8–10; Hebrews 11:6), whose work alone atones for our sin and merits eternal life for us. This is how we understand the words God spoke through His angel to a Gentile believer named Cornelius, as found in Acts 10:4: "Your prayers and your alms have ascended as a memorial before God." The reason God was pleased with Cornelius's prayers and gifts to the poor is that they flowed from his faith in the coming Christ, who alone had atoned for Cornelius's sin.

The Widow's Mite © CPH

Assisting after an earthquake in Chile/Erik M. Lunsford
Copyright © The Lutheran Church—Missouri Synod

Erik M. Lunsford
Copyright © The Lutheran Church—Missouri Synod

Christ, Our Treasure

God has given us an abundance of earthly prosperity. We Christians can enjoy God's good gifts without guilt. However, we must also take seriously Jesus' warning that we can easily be tempted to put our trust in wealth and worship it instead of God. We must also repent of the sinful notion that we are rich because we have impressed God with our good works and that He has rewarded us accordingly. We are all unworthy sinners who deserve nothing but God's wrath (see Ephesians 2:1–3), and so all we have from Him—especially forgiveness of sin and eternal life!—is pure, undeserved gift. We have complete forgiveness of our sins and the certain hope of eternal life because of Jesus' death and resurrection for us.

Even though we may not have a billion dollars to give away, and we don't run an international charity, our gifts have the highest value. As people who have been blessed with the riches of God's mercy in Christ, we have the joy and privilege of using the earthly gifts God has given us to help the poor and needy among us. We are free to perform acts of charity because we know our true treasure is Jesus! Therefore, we do our best to help those in need, because we know that God who loves us and saved us wants us to do this. However, we do not trust in our acts of charity to merit forgiveness and eternal life, because not only can we never love others as perfectly as we ought this side of heaven but also the very notion that our works can merit something from God is itself evil and mocks the atoning work of Christ for us. Instead, we live in daily repentance and faith in Christ—rejoicing in the forgiveness and eternal life Jesus has merited for us and then, in loving response to God's mercy, striving to serve others as God has served us in Christ.

© iStockphoto.com

© Jarrod Boord/Shutterstock, Inc.

Strength to Resist SIN

In 2008, Stanford University published a detailed "Prevention Guide" on the topic of slipping, tripping, and falling. The guide gives specific counsel on responsibilities, potential hazards, and controlling hazards since there are so many injuries from falling accidents each year.

In a similar way, Jesus son of Sirach gives us a useful "prevention guide" against falling into sin. He wrote:

> *Who will set a guard over my mouth and a seal of prudence upon my lips, in order that I may not fall on their account, and my tongue may not destroy me? O Lord, Father and Ruler of my life, do not abandon me to their counsel, and let me not fall because of them!*
>
> *Who will set whips over my thoughts and the discipline of wisdom over my heart, that they may not spare me in my errors of ignorance and that it may not pass over my sins; in order that my ignorant deeds may not be multiplied and my sins may not abound, so that I fall before my adversaries, and my enemy rejoices over me? O Lord, Father and God of my life, do not give me haughty eyes and remove from me all covetousness. Let neither gluttony nor lust overcome me and do not surrender me to a shameless soul.* (Ecclesiasticus 22:27–23:6)

This section of Ecclesiasticus is worth consideration and meditation from Christians, since we, too, struggle to avoid slipping into sin, tripping in our faith, and falling away. Its prayers are a wonderful example of how a believer today may pray to God for the strength to resist the desires of the sinful nature.

The Obstacle

Luther acknowledged that there was much good in the Book of Ecclesiasticus, and he encouraged its reading for devotional purposes. In Luther's preface to the book, he wrote:

> *This is a useful book for the ordinary man. The author concentrates all his effort on helping a citizen or housefather to be God-fearing, devout, and wise; and on showing what the relationship of such a man should be to God, the Word of God, priests, parents, wife, children, his own body, his servants, possessions, neighbors, friends, enemies, government, and anyone else. So one might well call this a book on home discipline or on the virtues of a pious householder. This indeed is the proper "spiritual discipline" and should be recognized as such. (AE 35:347–48)*

Ecclesiasticus 22:27–23:6 echoes teachings that we find in canonical Scripture. For example, the author of Ecclesiasticus says that he needs "a guard over [his] mouth," "whips over [his] thoughts," and "the discipline of wisdom over [his] heart." Such language echoes the words of Psalm 141:3–4:

> *Set a guard, O LORD, over my mouth; keep watch over the door of my lips! Do not let my heart incline to any evil, to busy myself with wicked deeds in company with men who work iniquity, and let me not eat of their delicacies!*

Scripture teaches that even though God has given believers new hearts and minds, which long to turn from sin and live according to His will (Ezekiel 36:26–27; Ephesians 2:8–10; Titus 2:11–14), we still have a sinful nature. Our hearts and minds are filled with sinful desires and thoughts with which we must struggle every day. (See Romans 7:14–25; Galatians 5:16–18; and Ephesians 4:21–24.) In Matthew 15:18–19, Jesus warns:

> *What comes out of the mouth proceeds from the heart, and this defiles a person. For out of the heart come evil thoughts, murder, adultery, sexual immorality, theft, false witness, slander.*

The Trip

"Pride goes before destruction, and a haughty spirit before a fall," Solomon wrote in Proverbs 16:18. With similar wisdom, Jesus son of Sirach asks God, "Do not give me haughty eyes"; that is, eyes that are instruments of a covetous, greedy heart. The son of Sirach is not teaching that God gives us such sinful desires. Instead, he is begging God not to abandon him to his own sinful desires but to rescue him from them, just as Jesus Christ taught us to pray, "Lead us not into temptation" (Matthew 6:13).

The Fall

Paul writes the following about hardened unbelievers: "And since they did not see fit to acknowledge God, God gave them up to a debased mind to do what ought not to be done" (Romans 1:28). Paul also is not teaching that God causes us to sin. Instead, Paul is teaching that if people refuse to repent, but insist on rebelling against God, He will eventually let them have their way—to their own destruction. Because of this truth, the writer of Ecclesiasticus begs God to rescue him from such a fate: "Remove from me all covetousness. Let neither gluttony nor lust overcome me and do not surrender me to a shameless soul" (23:5–6).

The Lord Will Raise You Up

When we fall into sin—and every believer does—we pray like King David, who wrote to the Lord:

Hide Your face from my sins, and blot out all my iniquities. Create in me a clean heart, O God, and renew a right spirit within me. Cast me not away from Your presence, and take not Your Holy Spirit from me. Restore to me the joy of Your salvation, and uphold me with a willing spirit. (Psalm 51:9–12)

David saw clearly that the Lord had to deliver him from sin and raise him up again to the new life that the Holy Spirit gives.

Today, when you stumble and fall, pray that you may fall into the loving arms of your Savior, who reaches out for you even now. Confessing your sins to the ruler of your life, receive discipline and His forgiveness. The heavenly Father is indeed the "God of [your] life" and the one who gives you life (Ecclesiasticus 23:4)! Like the loving father in the parable of the prodigal son, God will run to meet you, catch you in His arms, and bear you up!

The Books in Our Bibles

© Gord Horne/iStockphoto.com

Many church members have asked their pastors, "Why does the Roman Catholic Bible have extra books in the Old Testament?" The "extra books" they are referring to are known as the *Apocrypha*, a title that comes from a Greek word meaning "hidden" or "obscure." In 1546, the Roman Catholic Council of Trent made a list of biblical books they viewed as part of the canon of Scripture, and this list included the following books of the Apocrypha: Tobit, Judith, Fuller Esther, Wisdom of Solomon, Ecclesiasticus, Baruch (with Letter of Jeremiah), Fuller Daniel, 1 and 2 Maccabees. In contrast, most Bibles used by Protestants today do not contain these books of the Apocrypha. Why is this the case? Why some and not others?

If the books of the Apocrypha are new to you, know that they are not new to the Christian Church. They are part of a long-running discussion about the Bible. For example, the Apocrypha only went missing from most Protestant Bibles beginning in the 1820s! Rediscovering these books raises a host of long-standing questions. This article will summarize how Jews and Christians throughout history valued the Apocrypha. (The information below can be found in greater detail in the book *The Canon of Scripture* by F. F. Bruce.)

Canonical Views

There are four basic views of the value of the Apocrypha, which are typically described by the word *canon*, which is Greek for "rule" or "measure."

FULLY CANONICAL	DEUTEROCANONICAL
Books of the Apocrypha are like other books of the Bible.	Books of the Apocrypha are useful for doctrine and practice but do not have the same authority as other books of the Bible.

NON-CANONICAL	DANGEROUS
Books of the Apocrypha are useful for devotional and historical purposes but not for doctrine.	Books of the Apocrypha are too dangerous for Christians to read or study.

© Rasmus Rasmussen/iStockphoto.com

The Jewish Canon

The Jews of Jesus' day included the same books in their canon as we find in the Old Testament in most Protestant Bibles. In other words, they excluded the Apocrypha. Sometimes, the Jews of Jesus' day could refer to the entire Old Testament as "the Law" (cf. John 12:34). Other times, the entire Old Testament was referred to as "the Law and the Prophets" (cf. Matthew 7:12; Romans 3:21). However, most often, the Jews would divide the Old Testament into three sections:

DIVISION	BOOKS
The Law or Torah	Genesis, Exodus, Leviticus, Numbers, and Deuteronomy
The Prophets	Joshua, Judges, 1 and 2 Samuel, 1 and 2 Kings, Isaiah, Jeremiah, Ezekiel, Hosea, Joel, Amos, Obadiah, Jonah, Micah, Nahum, Habakkuk, Zephaniah, Haggai, Zechariah, Malachi
The Writings	Psalms, Proverbs, Job, Song of Songs, Ruth, Lamentations, Ecclesiastes, Esther, Daniel, Ezra, Nehemiah, 1 and 2 Chronicles

In Luke 24:44, Jesus refers to this three-fold division of the Old Testament common among the Jews of His day: "These are My words that I spoke to you while I was still with you, that everything written about Me in the Law of Moses and the Prophets and the Psalms must be fulfilled." (Here, Jesus uses the word "Psalms" as a synonym for "the Writings.") Some suggest that the Jewish Old Testament canon was not fixed until some rabbis made a decision about it at a meeting in Jamnia in AD 90. However, the rabbis at Jamnia at most discussed whether books such as the Song of Songs or Ecclesiastes should be part of the Old Testament canon, a discussion they could not have had if Jews up to that point did not recognize those books as already part of the Bible.

The Early Christian Church: East

The Early Church Fathers in Eastern Christianity had various views of the Apocrypha. In his Letter of Aristeas, Justin Martyr (c. AD 100–c. 165) discusses the origin of the Septuagint (the Greek translation of the Hebrew Old Testament), and he stresses that where the Septuagint differs from the Hebrew text (e.g., the Apocrypha contained in the Septuagint), this is evidence that the Hebrew text had been corrupted by the Jews so as to obscure the Scripture's clear prophetic testimony about Jesus. In contrast to Justin Martyr, Melito (d. c. 180), who was bishop of Sardis around 170, includes a list of Old Testament canonical books in a letter to his friend Onesimus—and this list is the same as the Old Testament canon used among the Jews of Jesus' day, with the exception of Melito's omission of the Book of Esther. Another Eastern Church Father, Origen (185–254), also recognized the same Old Testament canon as the Jews of Jesus' day—except that Origen included the apocryphal Letter of Jeremiah as part of Jeremiah. In the same way, Athanasius (297–373) followed the Hebrew canon of the Old Testament—except that he excluded Esther and included the apocryphal books Letter of Jeremiah and Baruch as part of Jeremiah. Finally, other Early Church Fathers in the East such as Cyril of Jerusalem (313–386), Gregory of Nazianzus (329–90), and Amphilochius (c. 339/340–c. 394/403) came to similar conclusions regarding the canon of the Old Testament.

The Early Christian Church: West

Even though Tertullian (c. 160–c. 225) nowhere gives a list of Old Testament canonical books, he quotes from various books of the Apocrypha in his writings as though they are part of the Old Testament canon. In contrast, Jerome (340/342–420) not only read the Greek Septuagint, but he also read the Hebrew Old Testament and accepted the same canon as the Jews of Jesus' day—thus rejecting the Apocrypha as canonical. Augustine (354–430), in contrast to Jerome, fully accepted the authority of the Apocrypha as part of the Old Testament canon. Augustine had great influence on the view of the Old Testament canon in Western Christianity—with the result that the Third Council of Carthage (397) and the Sixth Council of Carthage (419) both affirmed the Apocrypha as part of the Old Testament canon.

The Medieval and Reformation Eras

The two Wycliffite versions of the Bible in English (1384 and 1395) both included the Old Testament Apocrypha. But in the prologue to the second version, Wycliffe pointed out, following Jerome, that the Apocrypha should not be used to establish doctrine.

Martin Luther (1483–1546) agreed with Jerome in that he accepted the canon of the Old Testament commonly used among the Jews of Jesus' day. Luther also believed that the Apocrypha contained false teaching in conflict with the rest of the Old Testament. For example, 2 Maccabees 12:45 was used by Rome as a biblical basis for their teaching of purgatory and the practice of prayers for the dead. Even though Luther included the Apocrypha in his German translation of the Bible, he placed them at the end of the Old Testament as a kind of appendix.

Study Guide

COVER: The three archangels with Tobias, by Francesco Botticini. Art Archive, The / Art Archive, The

LifeLight

LifeLight Expands

Available NOW!

The Bible: An Overview
Genesis, Pt. 1
Genesis, Pt. 2
Exodus, Pt. 1
Exodus, Pt. 2
Wilderness Wanderings
Joshua
Judges
Ruth/Esther
1 & 2 Samuel
Life of David
1 & 2 Kings
1 & 2 Chronicles
Ezra/Nehemiah
Job
Selected Psalms
Proverbs
Ecclesiastes/ Song of Solomon
Isaiah, Pt. 1
Isaiah, Pt. 2
Jeremiah/Lamentations
Ezekiel
Daniel
Hosea/Joel/Amos
Obadiah/Jonah/Micah
Minor Prophets
Nahum/Habakkuk/ Zephaniah
Haggai/Zechariah/ Malachi
Matthew, Pt. 1
Matthew, Pt. 2
Mark
Luke, Pt. 1
Luke, Pt. 2
John, Pt. 1
John, Pt. 2
Acts, Pt. 1
Acts, Pt. 2
Romans, Pt. 1
Romans, Pt. 2
1 Corinthians
2 Corinthians
Galatians/Philippians/ Colossians
Ephesians/ 1 & 2 Thessalonians
Timothy/Titus/Philemon
Hebrews
James/Jude
1 & 2 Peter
1, 2, 3 John
Revelation

LifeLight Foundations

Baptism
Bible Feasts
Creation, New Creation
The Christian's Mission
End Times
Heaven & Hell
Law & Gospel
Ministry
Miracles
Parables
Prayer
Prophecy
Time between the Testaments
Triune God
Worship

Righteousness and Shame

Baruch; Letter of Jeremiah; Susanna

Distribute before session 1 for use in session 1.
Use enrichment magazine pp. 2–7.

Resources for Worship

Use these resources for your daily study at home and at the week's assembly.

Hymn

Entrust your days and burdens
To God's most loving hand;
He cares for you while ruling
The sky, the sea, the land.
For He who guides the tempests
Along their thund'rous ways
Will find for you a pathway
And guide you all your days.

Rely on God your Savior
And find your life secure.
Make His work your foundation
That your work may endure.
No anxious thought, no worry,
No self-tormenting care
Can win your Father's favor;
His heart is moved by prayer.

Take heart, have hope, my spirit,
And do not be dismayed;
God helps in ev'ry trial
And makes you unafraid.
Await His time with patience
Through darkest hours of night
Until the sun you hoped for
Delights your eager sight.

Leave all to His direction;
His wisdom rules for you
In ways to rouse your wonder
At all His love can do.
Soon He, His promise keeping,
With wonder-working pow'rs
Will banish from your spirit
What gave you troubled hours.

LSB 754:1–4

Prayer

Father, forgive us for our sins, washing us thoroughly in the blood of Your Son, our Savior, Jesus Christ. Lead us today and always by Your Holy Spirit to live wisely, according to Your Word. Keep us faithful in all trial and temptation, wiping away the deception of the world and the darkness of sin. Lift up our eyes from the present troubles to the day when You call us home, filling us with the sure and certain hope of our resurrection to eternal life through our Lord, Jesus Christ. Amen.

Digging Deep
My Personal Study for Week 1

Day 1 • Read Baruch 1:1–2:26

Since the Old Testament ends with the writings of prophets, it is fitting to begin with a book written in the style of the prophets and attributed to that time. The book could be among the earliest ones written during the Time between the Testaments. It continues the Old Testament themes of exile and repentance.

1. According to Jeremiah 36:4 and Baruch 1:1–2, who was Baruch?

The writer of the Book of Baruch is not the same person identified above but someone writing in his name and in a similar style.

2. Based on the assigned reading, what is the writer of Baruch trying to accomplish by writing his book?

3. We do not know precisely when the Book of Baruch was written. Its message fits broadly into the troubles the Israelites experienced following the Babylonian exile. According to Baruch 2:11–26, what needs did Baruch's readers have?

4. What can Baruch's prayer in 2:11–26 teach you about praying for your own circumstances?

5. *For personal reflection. Sharing optional.* List things for which you would ask God's forgiveness. Then write a prayer seeking His mercy and favor.

Day 2 • Read Baruch 2:27–4:4

6. Baruch 2:27–35 quotes God's promises to Moses. What message from the Sacred Scriptures did the writer cling to in his time of need? (Cf. Jeremiah 31:31–34 for help.)

7. What noticeable change do you see in the Book of Baruch at 3:9?

8. What Old Testament examples inspired the author of Baruch as he wrote 3:9–4:4?

9. a. What was the author of Baruch seeking?

b. How did he describe what he sought?

Day 3 • Read Baruch 4:5–5:9

10. What titles for God's people did the author of Baruch use in today's reading?

11. What can these titles teach us about his readers?

Gloriously Reveal the Works of God

Tobit; Ecclesiasticus 1:1–6:17

Distribute before session 2 for use in session 2.
Use enrichment magazine pp. 8–10.

Resources for Worship

Use these resources for your daily study at home and at the week's assembly.

Hymn

Your hand, O Lord, in days of old
Was strong to heal and save;
It triumphed over ills and death,
O'er darkness and the grave.
To You they came, the blind, the mute,
The palsied and the lame,
The lepers in their misery,
The sick with fevered frame.

O be our great deliv'rer still,
The Lord of life and death;
Restore and quicken, soothe and bless,
With Your life-giving breath.
To hands that work and eyes that see
Give wisdom's healing pow'r
That whole and sick and weak and strong
May praise You evermore.

LSB 846:1, 3

Prayer

Father, grant us wisdom to know and do Your will. Help us to do this out of gratitude and love for You, not for selfish gain. By the gift of Your Spirit, enable us to deny ourselves daily and follow Your Son, our Savior and Lord, so that Your love for others shines brightly through us. Rescue us from every trial, strengthen us against every temptation, and deliver us from all evil. In Jesus' holy name. Amen.

Digging Deep
My Personal Study for Week 2

Day 1 • Read Tobit 1–3

The Book of Tobit uniquely describes experiences of people exiled from the Northern Kingdom of Israel who wished to remain faithful to the Lord and His Word. However, the book also shows the effect of pagan beliefs and practices upon the Israelites living in exile during the Time between the Testaments.

1. Tobit is rich with drama and humor (be prepared to laugh out loud!). Although the story is fictional, the author places it in a historical setting, like works of historical fiction today. According to Tobit 1:1–4, 10–15, what setting does the author provide for his story?

Time

Place

Events

2. Read 2 Chronicles 30:1–12 and compare it with Tobit 1:3–9. What memory of the relationship between Judah (Southern Kingdom) and Israel (Northern Kingdom) does the writer of Tobit preserve?

3. According to Tobit 1:16–2:6; 3:1–3, how does Tobit describe his life and his motives/faith?

Life

Motives/Faith

4. Tobit's wife asks a key question for the book, one that was likely on the minds of Israelites in the years following the exile. How does her question (2:14) reveal the Israelites' concerns?

5. In chapter 3, the writer introduces a new element for his story; he connects the accounts of Tobit and Sarah by their prayers that their lives may end. However, read Philippians 1:18c–26. How does the apostle Paul offer a similar yet very different thought about death?

Day 2 • Read Tobit 4–8

6. Question 4 above points to a key question or concern of the Israelites in exile. How does Tobit's counsel to his son, Tobias, reveal Tobit's faith with respect to that question or concern? For help, read Tobit 4:5–11, 21.

7. Read Hebrews 10:32–39, which describes Christians also facing challenges.

a. By comparison, how does Tobit's faith speak the truth about the Lord?

b. How does it conflict with the biblical teaching described in Hebrews?

8. Tobit 5 introduces a new character.

a. Who is it?

b. What does he do?

c. How does he fulfill the faith and prayers of Tobit?

9. Summarize the remarkable plan that is proposed in Tobit 6:10–18.

10. **Challenge question**. Tobit 6–8 contains details of a Jewish custom and rite as practiced in the Time between the Testaments. Write an outline of the events for this custom and rite.

The Lord's Great Mercy

Ecclesiasticus 6:18–33:19

Distribute before session 3 for use in session 3.
Use enrichment magazine pp. 11–13.

Resources for Worship

Use these resources for your daily study at home and at the week's assembly.

Hymn

Jesus, priceless treasure,
Fount of purest pleasure,
Truest friend to me,
Ah, how long in anguish
Shall my spirit languish,
Yearning, Lord, for Thee?
Thou art mine,
O Lamb divine!
I will suffer naught to hide Thee;
Naught I ask beside Thee.

In Thine arms I rest me;
Foes who would molest me
Cannot reach me here.
Though the earth be shaking,
Ev'ry heart be quaking,
Jesus calms my fear.
Lightnings flash
And thunders crash;
Yet, though sin and hell assail me,
Jesus will not fail me.

Hence, all fear and sadness!
For the Lord of gladness,
Jesus, enters in.
Those who love the Father,
Though the storms may gather,
Still have peace within.
Yea, whate'er
I here must bear,
Thou art still my purest pleasure,
Jesus, priceless treasure!

LSB 743:1–2, 6

Prayer

Father, open our hearts and minds to Your Holy Spirit so that we might gain wisdom and understanding. Lift our eyes off this world to see You and find in Your Son, Jesus Christ, our Savior, the fullness of Your wisdom and power. Guide us so that we use our time wisely, living for You and the benefit of others. Fix our hearts on Jesus, the founder and perfecter of our faith. In His name. Amen.

Digging Deep
My Personal Study for Week 3

Day 1 • Read Ecclesiasticus 6:18–9:16

1. In what surprising way does Jesus son of Sirach describe wisdom in Ecclesiasticus 6:18–31?

2. Based on Ecclesiasticus 7:18–36, how does Jesus son of Sirach describe family relationships?

3. Jesus son of Sirach wrote his proverbs in a variety of styles, yet one style predominates.

a. What is the most common way he expresses his wise sayings?

b. What does this imply about his wisdom?

4. How did Jesus son of Sirach view women?

5. What does the advice in Ecclesiasticus 9:15–16 and 1 Thessalonians 2:11–13 teach about the value of the Scripture for your life?

Ecclesiasticus 9:15–16

1 Thessalonians 2:11–13

Day 2 • Read Ecclesiasticus 9:17–14:19

6. According to Ecclesiasticus 10:6–18, why is pride dangerous?

7. Compare Ecclesiasticus 11:18–19 with Jesus' parable in Luke 12:16–21. What wisdom do they teach?

8. Now compare Ecclesiasticus 12:7 with Matthew 5:43–48. How would you characterize the teaching of Jesus of Nazareth?

9. *For personal reflection. Sharing optional.* You've just been invited to dine with the leader of your nation. Chose a proverb in Ecclesiasticus 13:1–14:2 and explain why it is most helpful to you in that situation.

10. Contrast the sayings of Ecclesiasticus 14:11–19 with your hope as a Christian.

The Blessed Fear the Lord

Ecclesiasticus 33:20–51:30

Distribute before session 4 for use in session 4.
Use enrichment magazine pp. 14–17.

Resources for Worship

Use these resources for your daily study at home and at the week's assembly.

Hymn

Now thank we all our God
With hearts and hands and voices,
Who wondrous things has done,
In whom His world rejoices;
Who from our mothers' arms
Has blest us on our way
With countless gifts of love
And still is ours today.

Oh, may this bounteous God
Through all our life be near us,
With ever joyful hearts
And blessèd peace to cheer us
And keep us in His grace
And guide us when perplexed
And free us from all ills
In this world and the next!

All praise and thanks to God
The Father now be given,
The Son, and Him who reigns
With them in highest heaven,
The one eternal God,
Whom earth and heav'n adore;
For thus it was, is now,
And shall be evermore.

LSB 895

Prayer

Thank You, Father, for the gift of Your Word, Holy Scripture. Help us learn wisdom from Your Word and follow the example of those who served You faithfully in the past. Guide us by Your Holy Spirit to reflect the light of true wisdom, Jesus Christ, in all we say and do. Preserve us from all evil and lead us through all trial and temptation. In Jesus' name. Amen.

Digging Deep
My Personal Study for Week 4

Day 1 • Read Ecclesiasticus 33:20–36:31

1. Ecclesiasticus 33:25–33 gives contrasting advice. How does this use of contrast guide one toward wise decisions?

2. How does Ecclesiasticus 34:21–35:13 illustrate the role sacrifices played in the lives of God's people during the Time between the Testaments?

3. Ecclesiasticus 35:14–22a describes the relationship between sacrifices and prayers. Read also Luke 18:1–8. What valuable insight do these passages give you about your worship?

4. What reversal does Jesus son of Sirach pray for in Ecclesiasticus 36:13–19?

5. Reflect on Jesus son of Sirach's description of a wife's influences (Ecclesiasticus 36:27–31). What does this description say about the role of women in the Time between the Testaments?

Day 2 • Read Ecclesiasticus 37:1–39:11

6. According to Ecclesiasticus 37:7–15, what counselors should one heed or avoid?

Heed

Avoid

7. What sources of healing were available to persons in the Time between the Testaments (Ecclesiasticus 38:1–15)?

8. Explain why you do or do not believe that the advice in Ecclesiasticus 38:16–23 is realistic.

9. **Challenge question**. Many historians believed that ancient Jews rejected any use of images as idolatrous. But then archaeologists discovered paintings of biblical figures in a synagogue at Dura Europos (Syria) and depictions of them in many synagogue floor mosaics around the Middle East. Compare Ecclesiasticus 38:27c with Exodus 20:3–6. How were Jews interpreting Exodus 20:3–6 at this time in history?

10. What life did Jesus son of Sirach expect his readers to seek, according to Ecclesiasticus 38:34b–39:11?

Day 3 • Read Ecclesiasticus 39:12–42:14

11. Based on Jesus son of Sirach's hymn (39:12–35), summarize how he sees life (his "worldview").

Additions to Holy Scripture

Old Greek Esther; Prayer of Manasseh; Prayer of Azariah; The Song of the Three Holy Children; Bel and the Dragon

Distribute before session 5 for use in session 5.
Use enrichment magazine pp. 18–20.

Resources for Worship

Use these resources for your daily study at home and at the week's assembly.

Hymn

O bless the Lord, my soul!
Let all within me join
And aid my tongue to bless His name
Whose favors are divine.

O bless the Lord, my soul,
Nor let His mercies lie
Forgotten in unthankfulness
And without praises die!

'Tis He forgives thy sins;
'Tis He relieves thy pain;
'Tis He that heals thy sicknesses
And makes thee young again.

He crowns thy life with love
When ransomed from the grave;
He that redeemed my soul from hell
Hath sov'reign pow'r to save.

He fills the poor with good;
He gives the suff'rers rest.
The Lord hath judgments for the proud
And justice for th' oppressed.

His wondrous works and ways
He made by Moses known,
But sent the world His truth and grace
By His belovèd Son.

LSB 814

Prayer

Father, pour out Your Holy Spirit into our hearts to open our eyes so that we can see Your hand moving events in the world and in our lives toward salvation and hope. Help us always to trust You, even when we don't see the end of the problems we face. Teach us that You are always with us and that You are working all things for good in our lives and in the world. In Jesus' name. Amen.

Digging Deep
My Personal Study for Week 5

Day 1 • Read Old Greek Esther 11:2–13:18 or the following major additions to the book: 11:2–12; ch. 12; 13:1–7; 13:8–18

Old Greek Esther is the Hebrew version of Esther translated into Greek and then supplemented to enhance the story for readers of the Time between the Testaments. (The order of content may be different depending on which English translation you read. The chapter and verse divisions used here are found in the King James Version and the English Standard Version.)

1. What is the substance of Mordecai's dream (11:2–12)?

2. What action of Mordecai sparks the plot for the old Greek account of Esther?

3. According to Artaxerxes' letter, which was based on Haman's opinions, why were the Judeans regarded as a problem people, worthy of elimination (13:1–7)?

4. When Mordecai prayed, how did he explain his unwillingness to bow to Haman, a man in authority over Mordecai (13:8–14)?

5. What reasons did Mordecai give to the Lord for preserving Israel (13:15–18)?

Day 2 • Read Old Greek Esther 14:1–11:1 or the following major additions to the book: chs. 14–15; ch. 16; 11:1; read also the Prayer of Manasseh

6. a. In the Hebrew Book of Esther, there is no explicit mention of God. In contrast, what names for God do you find in Esther's prayer found in chapter 14 of Old Greek Esther?

b. How did Esther feel about the regal appointments of her office as queen?

7. Esther is recorded as approaching the king with considerable bravery in both the Hebrew and Greek accounts. But what happens in Old Greek Esther to evoke the king's compassion toward her?

8. What changes in government are considered wise, according to Artaxerxes' letter in chapter 16?

9. Second Chronicles 33:12–13, 18–19 mentions a prayer by Manasseh, king of Judah, that was recorded in a separate work. The fifteen verses of the Prayer of Manasseh present themselves as that prayer. How does this prayer describe God?

10. How do both Old Greek Esther and the Prayer of Manasseh speak to the issues and concerns of God's people during the Time between the Testaments?

Reverence the Divine Laws

2 Maccabees

Distribute before session 6 for use in session 6.
Use enrichment magazine pp. 21–22.

Resources for Worship

Use these resources for your daily study at home and at the week's assembly.

Hymn

Jerusalem the golden,
With milk and honey blest—
The promise of salvation,
The place of peace and rest—
We know not, oh, we know not
What joys await us there:
The radiancy of glory,
The bliss beyond compare!

Within those walls of Zion
Sounds forth the joyful song,
As saints join with the angels
And all the martyr throng.
The Prince is ever with them;
The daylight is serene;
The city of the blessèd
Shines bright with glorious sheen.

Around the throne of David,
The saints, from care released,
Raise loud their songs of triumph
To celebrate the feast.
They sing to Christ their leader,
Who conquered in the fight,
Who won for them forever
Their gleaming robes of white.

O sweet and blessèd country,
The home of God's elect!
O sweet and blessèd country
That faithful hearts expect!
In mercy, Jesus, bring us
To that eternal rest
With You and God the Father
And Spirit, ever blest.

LSB 672

Prayer

Father, thank You for the tabernacle You gave to Moses and the temple You built in Jerusalem as a place Your people could come and find You. Thank You for fulfilling the pattern of the temple in Your Son, our Savior, Jesus Christ, and in His sacrifice, which paid for our sins once and for all. Pour out upon us Your Holy Spirit so that we, the living stones built on the foundation of Christ Jesus, might share the Gospel and show Christ's love in all the places You have called us to serve. Amen.

Digging Deep
My Personal Study for Week 6

Day 1 • Read 2 Maccabees 1–3

The Book of 2 Maccabees is one of two histories that explain the rise of the Maccabees or Hasmoneans as leaders in Israel during the second century BC, when Israelites rebelled against the Seleucid Empire.

1. Two letters open 2 Maccabees (1:1–2:18). They were written to Jews in Egypt about the Feast of Booths, and they described the cleansing of the temple. What notorious events made that cleansing necessary?

2. According to 2 Maccabees 1:19–22, how was the altar fire restored at the temple in the days of Nehemiah?

3. According to 2 Maccabees 2, what acts of preservation did Jeremiah undertake before the fall of Jerusalem and the destruction of the temple by the Babylonians?

4. Based on 2 Maccabees 2:19–32, how and why was the book created?

How

Why

5. According to 2 Maccabees 3, how did the Lord protect the temple treasury when the Seleucid official Heliodorus came to "inspect" it?

Day 2 • Read 2 Maccabees 4–6

6. a. "Hellenization" in Jerusalem is mentioned in 2 Maccabees 4:13. What was hellenization?

b. Who introduced it?

7. Why was Onias, the former high priest, murdered?

8. Citizens of Jerusalem suffered under corrupt and greedy leadership. According to 2 Maccabees 5:1–14, what misunderstanding led King Antiochus to storm Jerusalem?

9. According to 2 Maccabees 5:15–20, why did the Lord allow Antiochus to profane the temple yet escape with his life?

10. One of 2 Maccabees's most important theological statements is found in 6:12–17. According to the passage, how does the Lord work in the lives of His people differently than He does with other nations?

Strength Comes from Heaven

1 Maccabees

Distribute before session 7 for use in session 7.
Use enrichment magazine pp. 23–26.

Resources for Worship

Use these resources for your daily study at home and at the week's assembly.

Hymn

Fight the good fight with all your might;
Christ is your strength, and Christ your right.
Lay hold on life, and it shall be
Your joy and crown eternally.

Cast care aside, lean on your guide;
His boundless mercy will provide.
Trust, and enduring faith shall prove
Christ is your life and Christ your love.

Faint not nor fear, His arms are near;
He changes not who holds you dear;
Only believe, and you will see
That Christ is all eternally.

LSB 664:1, 3–4

Prayer

Father, thank You for sending Your Son, Jesus Christ, to save us. Thank You for Your Holy Spirit, who brings us to new life in our Baptism and leads us in faith daily. Fill us with true zeal for You so that we boldly proclaim Your Gospel and follow in the footsteps of our Savior. Grant us wisdom to know Your will and courage and strength to do all to Your glory. In Jesus' holy name. Amen.

Digging Deep
My Personal Study for Week 7

Day 1 • Read 1 Maccabees 1–2

1. The Books of 1 and 2 Maccabees overlap somewhat in the history they provide, especially for describing the causes of the Jewish revolt and the leadership of Judas Maccabeus. As we learned in the previous session, 2 Maccabees begins with themes about the Feast of Booths and the temple. How does 1 Maccabees begin differently?

2. Read Daniel 11:29–32. How does 1 Maccabees describe fulfillment of this prophecy?

3. How would you characterize the prayer of Mattathias in 1 Maccabees 2:7–13?

4. Mattathias's actions are reminiscent of other Old Testament leaders. Summarize how his actions mirrored the actions of other heroes in Israel. (For help, see Exodus 32:25–29; Numbers 25:6–13; 1 Samuel 22:1–2.)

5. *For personal reflection. Sharing optional.* In 1 Maccabees 2:51–64, Mattathias cited eleven Old Testament examples in order to encourage his sons. Choose one example from Mattathias's list and explain why that figure is inspiring for you as a believer.

Day 2 • Read 1 Maccabees 3–5

6. According to Judas, what accounted for the success of his army? Read also Exodus 15:2–3.

7. Contrast how the Jews and the Gentiles sought divine insight regarding the coming battle near Jerusalem (1 Maccabees 3:48). Should Christians today follow the example of the Jews in this passage? Explain your answer.

8. What testimony did Judas believe his victories would bear before the Gentiles?

9. What was the condition of the temple courts when the Maccabees recovered it?

10. Judas and his brothers achieved more than they could have imagined when they first took up arms in 1 Maccabees 2. In about four years, they conquered much of the territory that was ancient Israel. What dangers do you foresee for these brothers at this point in the history?

Day 3 • Read 1 Maccabees 6–9

11. Contrast the way the writer described Antiochus Epiphanes in 1 Maccabees 1:41–64 with how he described himself in 6:10–12. What does this contrast illustrate about human nature?

12. In 1 Maccabees 7:17, the writer cites Psalm 79:3 as a prophecy about Alcimus's treachery. According to 1 Maccabees 9:54–57, how were the prophecies of the psalm finally fulfilled in the life of Alcimus?

13. a. Can a Christian rightly say the prayer in 1 Maccabees 7:38?

The Lord Foiled Them by the Hand of a Woman

Judith

Distribute before session 8 for use in session 8.
Use enrichment magazine pp. 27–29.

Resources for Worship

Use these resources for your daily study at home and at the week's assembly.

Hymn

God moves in a mysterious way
His wonders to perform;
He plants His footsteps in the sea
And rides upon the storm.

Judge not the Lord by feeble sense,
But trust Him for His grace;
Behind a frowning providence
Faith sees a smiling face.

His purposes will ripen fast,
Unfolding ev'ry hour;
The bud may have a bitter taste,
But sweet will be the flow'r.

You fearful saints, fresh courage take;
The clouds you so much dread
Are big with mercy and will break
In blessings on your head.

LSB 765:1–3, 5

Prayer

Father, guide us by Your Holy Spirit as we face the challenges that confront us every day. Anchor us in Jesus Christ, and instruct us by Your Word so that we stand in faith no matter what the circumstance. Keep us faithful to You, protected from every temptation and strengthened in every trial by Your promise and presence. Remind us that You are always faithful, providing a way through or around every obstacle (1 Corinthians 10:13). Amen.

Digging Deep
My Personal Study for Week 8

Day 1 • Read Judith 1:1–3:8

The Book of Judith purports to be written during the Assyrian conquest of Israel but was clearly written much later.

1. What effect, what impression, do the opening words (1:1–6) have on you as a reader?

2. How did the people in the western regions regard Nebuchadnezzar's request (1:7–11)?

3. Based on Judith 2, what sort of person was Holofernes?

4. How did the people in Holofernes's path receive him and his message (2:28–3:4)?

5. What unique order in Judith 3 will set Holofernes in direct conflict with the Judeans and their God? Read also Isaiah 43:10–13.

Day 2 • Read Judith 3:9–6:21

6. Compare events in 2 Kings 24:10–14 with Judith 4:2–3. The Book of Judith includes a historical mistake in this passage. Record the writer's mistake, which leads historians to regard the book as fiction.

7. In Judith 4:8, what details about leadership help us date the book more accurately? (Hint: remember what you learned about Israel in 1 Maccabees.)

8. How did the people in Jerusalem seek God's intervention (4:9–12)?

9. According to Achior in chapter 5, how could the Judeans be defeated?

10. How did the Assyrians respond to Achior's report (ch. 6)?

Day 3 • Read Judith 7–9

11. The Edomites, Moabites, and coastland people give war counsel to Holofernes (7:1–18).

a. What did they counsel?

b. How did it affect the people of Bethulia?

12. What words of faith and prophecy did Uzziah speak to the people (7:19–32)?

Wisdom Is Radiant and Unfading

Wisdom of Solomon

Distribute before session 9 for use in session 9.
Use enrichment magazine pp. 30–32.

Resources for Worship

Use these resources for your daily study at home and at the week's assembly.

Hymn

Come, you faithful, raise the strain
Of triumphant gladness!
God has brought His Israel
Into joy from sadness,
Loosed from Pharaoh's bitter yoke
Jacob's sons and daughters,
Led them with unmoistened foot
Through the Red Sea waters.

'Tis the spring of souls today:
Christ has burst His prison
And from three days' sleep in death
As a sun has risen;
All the winter of our sins,
Long and dark, is flying
From His light, to whom is giv'n
Laud and praise undying.

Alleluia! Now we cry
To our King immortal,
Who, triumphant, burst the bars
Of the tomb's dark portal.
Come, you faithful, raise the strain
Of triumphant gladness!
God has brought His Israel
Into joy from sadness!

LSB 487:1–2, 5

Prayer

Father, keep us faithful through all the trials and temptations of this life. Anchor us by Your Holy Spirit in Jesus Christ, our Good Shepherd, so that the cares and pressures of this world do not distract or discourage us. Wipe away deception from our eyes and fear from our hearts, filling us with the spirit of power, love, and sound thinking we need to witness to You, the one true God. In Jesus' name. Amen.

Digging Deep
My Personal Study for Week 9

Day 1 • Read Wisdom of Solomon 1:1–4:19

The Wisdom of Solomon was most likely the last of the Apocrypha to be written and was definitely composed in Greek. It likely reflects the concerns of Jews living in Ptolemaic Egypt nearer the time of Christ.

1. According to chapter 1, what are the origins of life and death?

Life

Death

2. What counsel do the ungodly offer to one another in chapter 2?

3. Contrast the destinies of the righteous and the ungodly. How do their futures differ?

4. The brief story in Genesis 5:22–24 is fleshed out in Wisdom of Solomon 4:10–15. How does this retelling of the story illustrate what Jews thought about righteousness in the Time between the Testaments?

5. Wisdom is mentioned in Wisdom of Solomon 1:4, 6; 3:11; and 4:17. Based on these initial passages, how is the book defining wisdom?

Day 2 • Read Wisdom of Solomon 4:20–8:21

6. Wisdom of Solomon 5:8–14 comments in picturesque language about the folly of arrogance and boasting. Which illustration best captures your experience with such folly?

7. According to Wisdom of Solomon 6:1–11, why did the author write his book?

8. In Hebrew and Greek, the common terms for *wisdom* are grammatically feminine, which led Israelite writers to describe wisdom as a woman. How does one love wisdom?

9. In 1 Corinthians 1:24, 30, the apostle Paul describes Christ as our wisdom. Wisdom of Solomon 7:25–27 speaks somewhat differently. What features of this passage point to a different person as wisdom during the Time between the Testaments?

10. *For personal reflection. Sharing optional.* Wisdom has many benefits. Wisdom of Solomon 7:22b–23 lists no fewer than twenty-one benefits, and there are others mentioned throughout today's reading! Choose three benefits that you feel are most needed for your life right now.

Day 3 • Read Wisdom of Solomon 9–12

11. Solomon is never mentioned by name in the book titled the "Wisdom of Solomon." What details in the prayer of chapter 9 reveal that the author indeed had Solomon in mind? For help, see 1 Kings 3:5–15.

12. Wisdom of Solomon 10:1–14 celebrates wisdom appearing throughout the Book of Genesis. Identify the person described for each reference.

v. 1 v. 3 v. 4

v. 5 v. 6 v. 10

v. 13

13. In what just way did the Lord punish the Egyptians, according to Wisdom of Solomon 11:15–16?

14. Wisdom of Solomon 11:21–12:2 is an interlude that departs from the writer's review of Old Testament history. Based on this interlude, what is God like?

15. According to Wisdom of Solomon 12:19–22, what lessons should we draw from the stories of the Old Testament? Consult 1 Corinthians 10:1–6.

Day 4 • Read Wisdom of Solomon 13:1–15:17

16. Compare Wisdom of Solomon 13:1-9 with Paul's comments in Romans 1:18–25. List points of agreement you find.

17. What point does the apostle make that Wisdom of Solomon does not?

18. While reading Wisdom of Solomon 13:10–19, a point of irony may have struck you as most humorous. Should Christians today use such irony and humor in attempts to advance the faith? Explain your answer.

19. Consider Wisdom of Solomon 14:27. Based on your knowledge of Scripture and life, is this statement true or false? Explain your answer.

20. What does knowing God mean, according to Wisdom of Solomon 15:1–3?

Day 5 • Read Wisdom of Solomon 15:18–19:22

21. What insightful commentary does Wisdom of Solomon 16:5–8 provide for Numbers 21:5–9? (Cf. also John 3:14–15.)

22. What does creation teach, according to Wisdom of Solomon 16:24–26?

23. What is fear, according to Wisdom of Solomon 17:12?

24. How does Wisdom of Solomon 18:9 reflect the values of the Jews during the Time between the Testaments?

25. How does the writer characterize the wonders God performed for the exodus in Wisdom of Solomon 19:6, 18–21?

13. In chapter 8, we finally meet the heroine and namesake of the book. Who was Judith?

14. Contrast the faith of Judith with the faith of the elders. Which expression best reflects your faith during a crisis?

15. In Judith's prayer (ch. 9), she appeals to God for help in some surprising ways.

a. Write an example that most surprised you.

b. Describe why it surprised you.

Day 4 • Read Judith 10:1–13:11

16. Based on Judith 10:1–5, what was Judith's strategy?

17. How did the Assyrians respond to Judith (10:11–19)?

18. What did Judith promise Holofernes that greatly pleased him?

19. a. Judith made special preparations for her stay among the Assyrians (12:1–9). What were her preparations?

b. Why were they important?

20. a. In 13:4–16, how did Judith address God?

b. How did she see evidence of His presence in her words?

Day 5 • Read Judith 13:11–16:25

21. When Judith returned triumphant to Bethulia, she and Uzziah celebrated her victory and her virtue. What points about her virtue did they celebrate?

22. Achior the Ammonite reenters the story (ch. 14). What role does he now play?

23. The 1949 Geneva Convention established international standards for humanitarian treatment during war. Modern militaries operate by "rules of engagement." However, the story of Judith lends credence to a popular English proverb, "All is fair in love and war." Do you believe this proverb is true? Explain your answer.

24. Judith's hymn of praise (ch. 16) includes major themes of war and creation. Given the story, the theme of war easily makes sense. Why would Judith's hymn include the theme of creation?

25. In 16:21–25, Judith displays a number of virtues that must have been important to the author of the story. What virtues does he cite to illustrate her strength of character?

b. Why or why not?

14. Judas, the great military leader of a renewed kingdom of Israel, made a decision with unforeseen consequences in 1 Maccabees 8.

a. What was Judas's decision?

b. What would be its outcome?

15. a. Who emerged as the next leader for Israel?

b. How did he gain leadership?

Day 4 • Read 1 Maccabees 10–12

16. After the death of Judas, 1 Maccabees expands the scope of its history to describe broader and broader developments around the eastern Mediterranean region rather than focus exclusively on Israel. The writing also becomes less spiritual and less military, focusing increasingly on politics and alliances. A new development arises in Israel's governance. What happens with Jonathan?

17. a. Who is the famous historical figure who appears in Israel's history, as described in 1 Maccabees 10:57–58; 11:8–12?

b. What role is this person playing at this point?

18. Jonathan is described in 1 Maccabees 11 as between the warring forces of the Seleucids (Syria) and the Ptolemies (Egypt), as had happened to so many leaders of Israel before. How does Jonathan fare?

19. Alliances at times bring together rather odd situations. Based on 1 Maccabees 12:9–12, 20–23, what was the relationship between the pagan Spartans and the Israelites?

20. Reflect on this relationship and on Paul's counsel in 2 Corinthians 6:14–7:1. What lessons would you draw from it for your own life and alliances?

Day 5 • Read 1 Maccabees 13–16

21. What monumental achievement did God's people observe in the "170th year" (13:41)?

22. According to the poem in 1 Maccabees 14:4–15, what characterized the rule of Simon?

23. Earlier, we noted that the content of 1 Maccabees became more political and less spiritual as it went on. How is this change illustrated in the poem about Simon?

24. Contrast the battle preparation of 1 Maccabees 3:44–60 with Simon's speech in 16:2b–3. What changes do you see?

25. Every history needs a focus. The writer of 1 Maccabees displays that focus in the way he ends his book. Contrast the ending focus of 1 Maccabees with that of Nehemiah (13:29–31), one of the last histories written for the Old Testament. How do they differ in focus?

Day 3 • Read 2 Maccabees 7–9

11. *For personal reflection. Sharing optional.* Second Maccabees 6:18–7:42 famously describes the deaths of God's people who refused to abandon the Law of Moses and embrace hellenization. Write how these accounts affect you as a believer.

12. Our English word *martyr* comes from a Greek word meaning "to bear witness" (a form of that Greek word appears in 2 Maccabees 7:6). What witness/testimony about the Lord did the seven brothers provide to their tormentors?

13. How did their mother bear witness?

14. Read Hebrews 11:35–37. How is the observance of feast days for martyrs a benefit to you and other Christians today?

15. A great hero of the Time between the Testaments is introduced in 2 Maccabees 8.

a. Who was he?

b. What did he accomplish?

Day 4 • Read 2 Maccabees 10–12

16. What prayers and observances accompanied the purification of the temple?

Prayers

Observances

17. According to 2 Maccabees 10:28–38, how was the army of the Maccabees different from that of Timothy (Seleucids)?

18. The letter at 2 Maccabees 11:34–38 tells us more about the change of heart Lysias and other Seleucids experienced. Contrast the reasons for this change in 11:13 with those in 11:34–38.

19. How does 2 Maccabees 12 describe the Lord?

20. **Challenge question.** In 2 Maccabees 12:39–45, Judas made a surprising discovery and proposed a surprising solution, which in later Church history inspired false teachings about purgatory. Read Hebrews 9:27. How does the solution offered by Judas conflict with New Testament teaching about God's judgment?

Day 5 • Read 2 Maccabees 13–15

21. Based on 2 Maccabees 15, how would you describe Judas as a leader?

22. Based on 2 Maccabees 14, what qualities of friendship do you find in Alcimus, the former high priest, and in Nicanor, the Seleucid commander?

Alcimus

Nicanor

23. The story of Razis (2 Maccabees 14:37–46) presents us with a dilemma. Was the death of Razis noble (cf. v. 42) or not? Explain your answer.

24. What was the substance of Judas's dream/vision?

25. The writer of 2 Maccabees ends his book on a high note: the victory of Judas over Nicanor. He also includes a comparison of his work with beverages. From your perspective as a believer today, is the Book of 2 Maccabees "harmful to drink" or "delicious . . . enjoyment" for the soul? Explain your answer.

Day 3 • Read Daniel 3:13–23 and the Prayer of Azariah

11. The Prayer of Azariah is found in Greek versions of Daniel after 3:23 of that book. How does this prayer supplement the story as told in the Hebrew Book of Daniel?

12. What facts about God does the author of the prayer wish to establish in Prayer of Azariah 1–8?

13. How does the prayer appeal to God for mercy?

14. What historical situation is assumed by the author in Prayer of Azariah 14–15?

15. The author of the Prayer of Azariah has a message he wishes to share with the world (vv. 21–22). Contrast his message with Jesus' message in Matthew 28:18–20. How are the messages different?

Day 4 • Read the Song of the Three Holy Children

16. In verses 23–27, how does the writer for the Song of the Three Holy Children explain the survival of Azariah and the others in the furnace?

17. The prayer is a *benediction,* which repeats the word "blessed." What distinguishes verses 29–34 of the Song of the Three Holy Children from the rest of the prayer?

18. In view of the story in Daniel, how is the benediction of the Song of the Three Holy Children in verse 44 ironic?

19. How do verses 60–65 of the Song of the Three Holy Children reveal an Old Testament hierarchy for the lives of the people at that time?

20. What hope or confidence does this prayer inspire in you as a worshiper of the one true God?

Day 5 • Read Bel and the Dragon

21. Bel and the Dragon are two similar stories found at the end of Greek editions of the Book of Daniel. What challenge introduces the story of Bel?

22. Both the priests of Bel and Daniel exhibit confidence. What is the basis of the confidence for each of them?

Priests of Bel

Daniel

23. How does Daniel overcome the priests of Bel in the matter of the temple and in the matter of the dragon?

Temple

Dragon

24. The stories of Bel and the Dragon end in a way that is familiar to readers of the Bible. What irony do you see in verses 32 and 37?

25. A promise of God inspired Daniel's faith. How does the promise behind Daniel's comments in verse 38 of Bel and the Dragon encourage you to face the "lions" that surround you?

12. Explain why you agree or disagree with Jesus son of Sirach's conclusions about the joys of life (40:18–27).

13. Contrast Ecclesiasticus 41:1–4 with Paul's teaching in 1 Corinthians 15:51–57. How does the Christian message speak differently?

14. In Ecclesiasticus 41:15–42:8, Jesus son of Sirach lists causes of proper shame and things that should not make one ashamed. What place does shame have in the life of a Christian?

15. Is Ecclesiasticus 42:14a true or false? Explain your answer.

Day 4 • Read Ecclesiasticus 42:15–46:20

16. What great theme is taken up in 42:15–43:33?

17. How might the statement "He is the all" (43:27) be misunderstood or rightly understood?

Misunderstood

Understood

18. Skim Ecclesiasticus 44:1–50:21. How would you characterize this section of the book?

19. A famous Old Testament figure is missing from Ecclesiasticus 44.

a. Based on verses 3–7, who was this figure?

b. Why was this figure left out?

20. One character receives more attention than the others in Ecclesiasticus 44:16–46:20.

a. Who is that character?

b. Why does he receive more attention?

Day 5 • Read Ecclesiasticus 47–51

21. What special blessing does the account of Elijah (48:1–11) contain?

22. Why are Hezekiah and Isaiah treated together (48:17–25)?

23. In today's reading, one figure receives more attention than all the others.

a. Who is that figure?

b. Why does he receive more attention?

24. From your perspective, is the prayer of 51:1–12 an appropriate prayer that one could use today? Explain your answer.

25. Reflect on the closing poem about wisdom (51:13–30). Choose a passage of the poem and rewrite it in view of 1 Corinthians 1:24, 30.

Day 3 • Read Ecclesiasticus 14:20–20:31

11. With what imagery does Ecclesiasticus 15:1–10 personify wisdom?

12. How does Jesus son of Sirach describe responsibility for sin (Ecclesiasticus 15:11–20)?

13. Ecclesiasticus 16:1–5 includes a personal reflection that describes circumstances in Israel during the late third century BC or early second century BC. What was Jesus son of Sirach's experience?

14. Based on your knowledge of the Old Testament, to whom does Jesus son of Sirach compare the Israelites of his day in Ecclesiasticus 16:7–10?

15. "How great is the mercy of the Lord, and His forgiveness for those who turn to Him!" (Ecclesiasticus 17:29). How would you as a Christian answer this exultant question/declaration?

Day 4 • Read Ecclesiasticus 21–27

16. Contrast Ecclesiasticus 21:3 with Hebrews 4:12–16. How do the swords differ in their consequences depending on the one who wields them?

17. What does Ecclesiasticus 21:26 mean? (Consider the context for help.)

18. What sad history perhaps lies behind Jesus son of Sirach's comments in Ecclesiasticus 22:3–6?

19. *For personal reflection. Sharing optional.* Recite the prayer in Ecclesiasticus 22:27–23:6 and write how it speaks to the needs of your life today.

20. Read Ecclesiasticus 25:16–26:18 in view of the Christ-based wisdom in Ephesians 5:25–33. How does the wisdom of the New Testament compare?

Day 5 • Read Ecclesiasticus 27:30–33:19

21. How does God repay slander? (See Ecclesiasticus 28:14–15.)

22. Ecclesiasticus 29:1–20 describes relations between neighbors. Explain why you agree or disagree with Jesus son of Sirach's description of what it means to be a good neighbor.

23. What are the essentials of life for this writer in the Time between the Testaments? (See Ecclesiasticus 29:21.)

24. What are the blessings and curses of wealth, according to Ecclesiasticus 31:1–11?

25. *For personal reflection. Sharing optional.* "Providence" is about how God provides for all our needs in life. Read Ecclesiasticus 32:14–33:6 and write a prayer of thanks to God for His provident care for you.

Day 3 • Read Tobit 9–12

11. Here we see the biblical practice of parents blessing their children, from which parents today may learn ways to care for their children. How did Raguel and Tobit offer blessings to/for Tobias and Sarah?

Tobias

Sarah

12. *For personal reflection. Sharing optional.* How has the triune God blessed you?

Father

Son

Holy Spirit

13. Read Deuteronomy 18:10–11 and write your reflections on the role given to magic in Tobit 6:17–18; 11:7–13a.

14. **Challenge question.** Summarize what the Book of Tobit teaches about angels. *Note well that some points in Tobit are contrary to passages in Scripture.*

15. Tobit 12:9a makes a bold doctrinal statement. In view of the Gospel of Jesus Christ, describe how you agree or disagree with Tobit's statement.

Day 4 • Read Tobit 13–14

16. According to Tobit's thanksgiving prayer, why should one bless God?

17. Tobit 13:8–18 provides a focus for the thanks and joy of God's people. According to Tobit, why is this focus important? Read also Isaiah 2:1–5.

18. **Challenge question**. Tobit's closing speech to Tobias likely records things as prophecy that had already taken place when the author wrote the book (14:4–5a). It also includes a prophecy about the future of Jerusalem (14:5b–7). Based on your knowledge of biblical history, explain how Tobit's prophecy in 14:5b–7 was or was not fulfilled.

19. Tobit closes by revisiting a theme (14:10, 11b–13) repeated throughout the book. Given the history of the Time between the Testaments, why would this theme be so important to Israelites of that era?

20. The Book of Tobit includes numerous prayers and praises (3:2–6; 3:11–15; 8:5–8; 8:15–17; 11:14–15; ch. 13). Select a favorite from this list and explain why you favor it.

Day 5 • Read Ecclesiasticus 1:1–6:17

Among the books of the Apocrypha, Ecclesiasticus is the only one that names the historical author of the book and why he wrote it.

21. According to the prologue, written by the grandson of Jesus son of Sirach, why was it important to write and preserve this book?

22. According to Jesus son of Sirach, how has wisdom come to you?

23. Jesus son of Sirach repeatedly chooses one phrase to describe the wise in Ecclesiasticus 1–2.

a. What is that phrase?

b. What does it mean?

24. Jesus Christ taught that one becomes a son of God through the Holy Spirit's work in Baptism (John 3:3–8). According to Jesus son of Sirach, how does one become a son of the Most High (Ecclesiasticus 4:10)?

25. *For personal reflection. Sharing optional.* What wisdom regarding repentance in Ecclesiasticus 5:1–7 do you find most helpful for you personally?

12. What titles does the author of Baruch use for God?

13. What can these titles teach us about the author's relationship to God?

14. Think about your life circumstances.

a. What titles best describe you?

b. What titles best describe your relationship to the Lord?

Day 4 • Read the Letter of Jeremiah

15. *For personal reflection. Sharing optional.* Just as the author of Baruch attributed his writing to an earlier biblical figure, the author of the Letter of Jeremiah attributed his work to an earlier prophet. What message does the author of this letter have for his readers?

16. The Letter of Jeremiah has a unique style. How does the writer get his point across repeatedly?

17. a. Record your favorite example of the author's style.

b. Summarize why it is your favorite.

18. How does the Letter of Jeremiah illustrate the worries and needs of God's people living after the time of the exile?

Day 5 • Read Susanna

19. The Book of Baruch and the Letter of Jeremiah created the setting for their writings from the time of the Babylonian exile and the writings in the Book of Jeremiah. What setting and source of inspiration stands behind the story of Susanna?

Setting

Source of inspiration

20. What problems faced by God's people are addressed in this well-crafted short story?

21. What positive, helpful messages do you discover in reading this story?

22. How does the Lord rescue Susanna?

23. How do God's means for rescuing Susanna move you to patience and trust in your life as a believer? Read also Romans 8:31–39.

Patience

Trust

In Luther's prefaces to the Apocrypha, he stressed that the books of the Apocrypha were useful for devotional and historical purposes but were not to be seen as equal to the other Old Testament books. So he would not use them to establish doctrine.

Various versions of the Bible among future Reformed Christians took the same approach to the Apocrypha as Luther. In the 1800s, some Reformed theologians rejected the Apocrypha completely and did not include it in their editions of Holy Scripture. This negative view of the Apocrypha among some Reformed Christians has influenced most versions of the Bible in English used by Protestants today in that these versions of the Bible do not contain the Apocrypha.

Summary

As you are learning from this LifeLight study, the writings of the Apocrypha provide valuable insights about the Time between the Testaments and about what would happen in the New Testament. For those reasons alone, they are valuable to read.

God Rescues Us

In 2006, there emerged in Iraq a group of Sunni Muslims who took terror and violence in a new direction. The Islamic State in Iraq and Syria (ISIS) grew stronger and more bold as moderate Sunnis, who felt persecuted by Iraqi Shia Muslims, organized resistance. They set a goal of founding an Islamic caliphate governed under Sharia law. As ISIS gained power, they targeted Christians with persecution and beheadings. Although Christians in the Middle East have survived alongside Muslims since the seventh century, and have even enjoyed seasons of peace, they now face a new and murderous threat.

God will eventually rescue believers from evil forces that oppose Him and His children. This will happen, ultimately, at the second coming of God's Son. Until then, we must understand that Jesus had to first rescue us from our greatest enemy: our own sin that separated us from God.

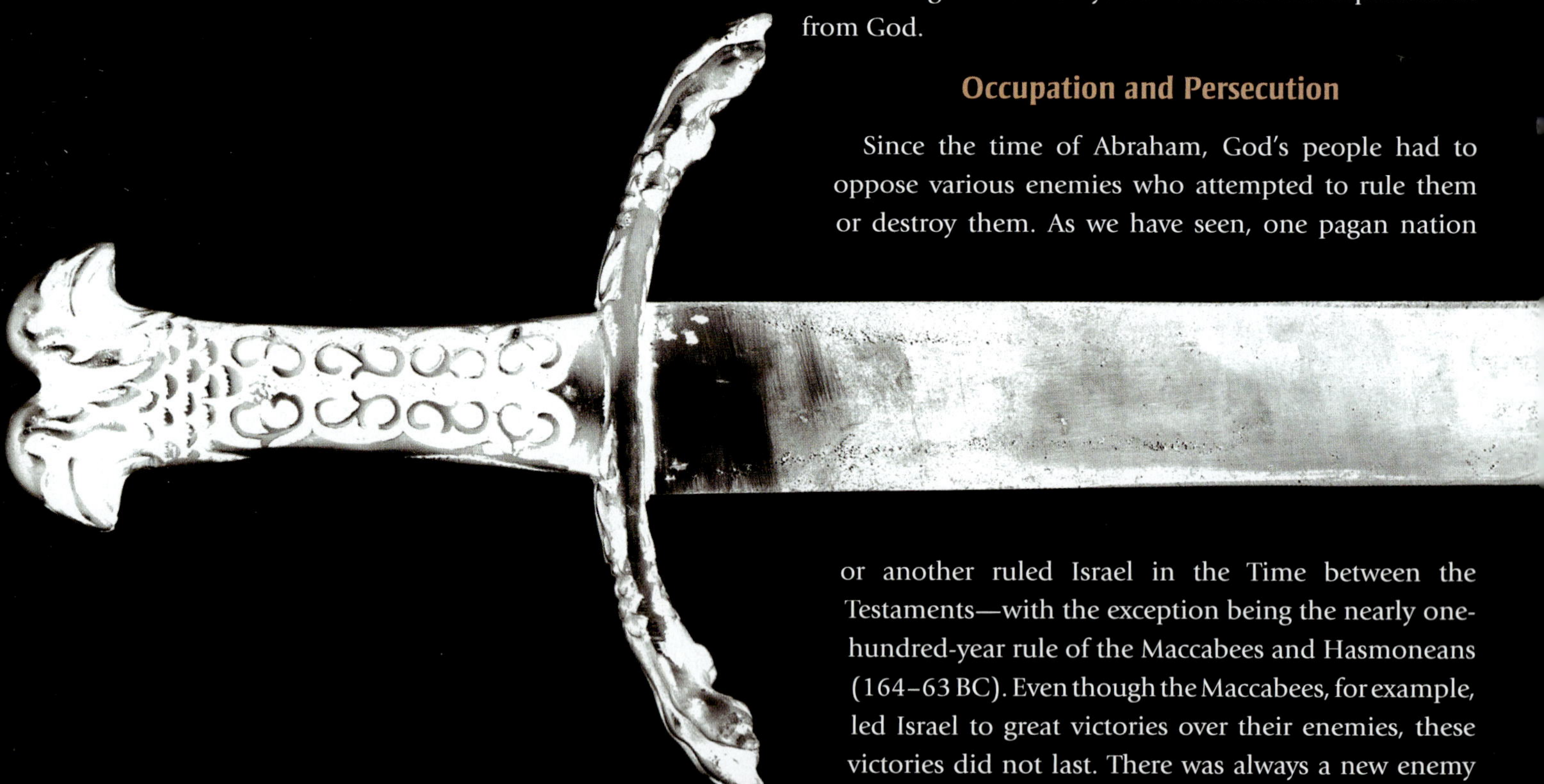

Occupation and Persecution

Since the time of Abraham, God's people had to oppose various enemies who attempted to rule them or destroy them. As we have seen, one pagan nation or another ruled Israel in the Time between the Testaments—with the exception being the nearly one-hundred-year rule of the Maccabees and Hasmoneans (164–63 BC). Even though the Maccabees, for example, led Israel to great victories over their enemies, these victories did not last. There was always a new enemy who would attempt to rule them and oppress them.

Due to the many foreign occupations, God's people longed for the time when the Messiah would appear and rescue them from their enemies. We think of Zechariah, father of John the Baptist, who prayed the following:

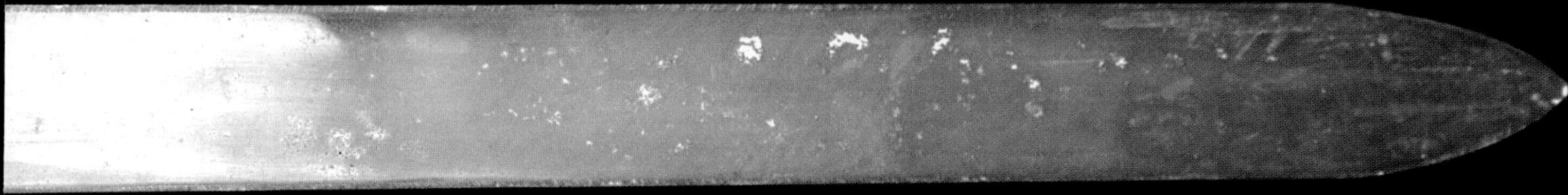

God sent His Son into this world to suffer and die for His enemies that we might be forgiven and become His dearly loved children (see Romans 3:9–31; 5:1–11; Ephesians 2:1–10; Colossians 1:21–23).

Now that God has rescued us from our own rebellion against Him, we can rejoice in being His redeemed people. We may face persecution in this world from those who insist on hating God and His children. Sometimes God may deliver us from our earthly enemies and give us times of peace and freedom, as God's people experienced during the time of the Maccabees. We can read about examples of God giving such earthly victories to His people in Hebrews 11:29–35a.

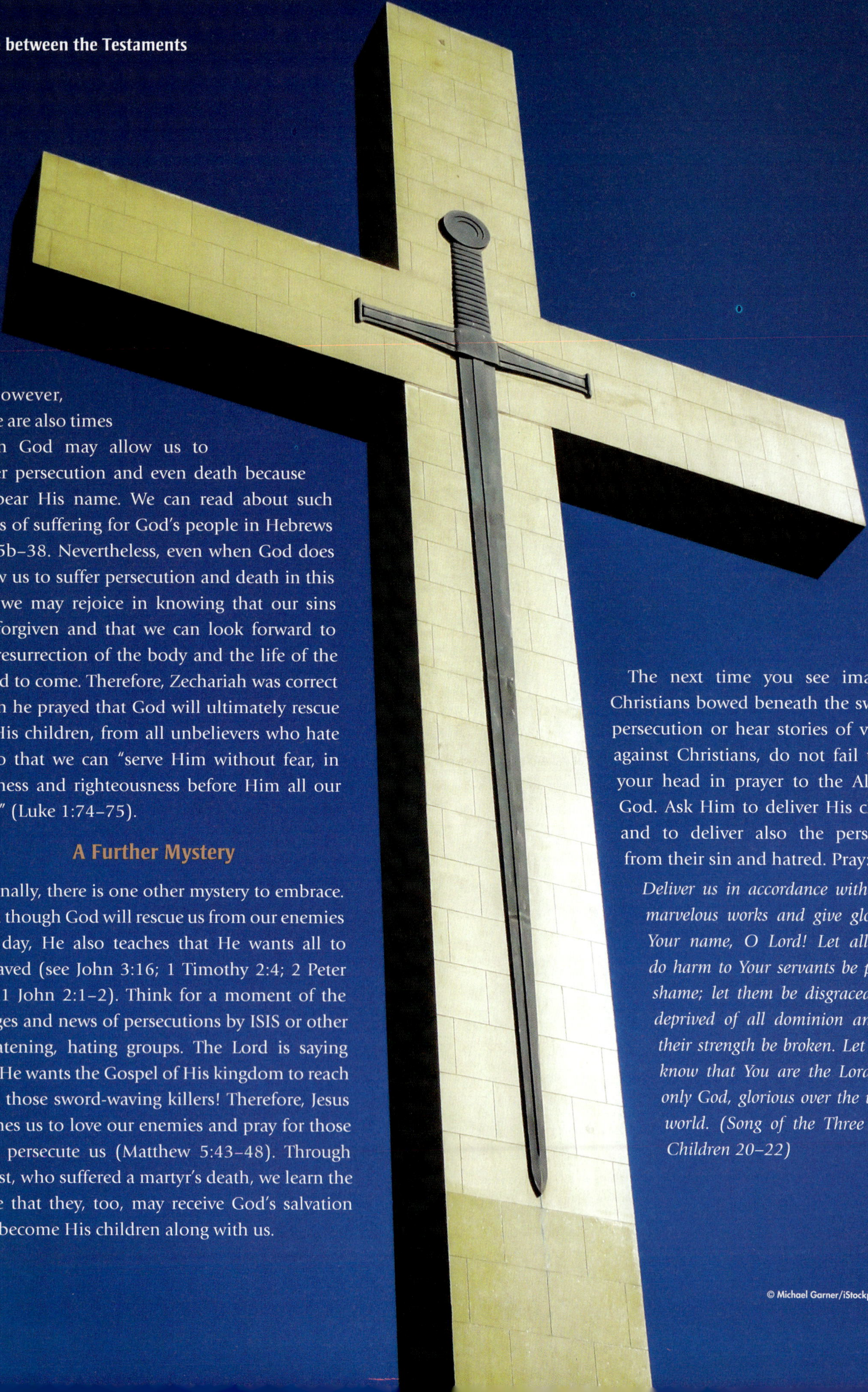

However, there are also times when God may allow us to suffer persecution and even death because we bear His name. We can read about such times of suffering for God's people in Hebrews 11:35b–38. Nevertheless, even when God does allow us to suffer persecution and death in this life, we may rejoice in knowing that our sins are forgiven and that we can look forward to the resurrection of the body and the life of the world to come. Therefore, Zechariah was correct when he prayed that God will ultimately rescue us, His children, from all unbelievers who hate us so that we can "serve Him without fear, in holiness and righteousness before Him all our days" (Luke 1:74–75).

A Further Mystery

Finally, there is one other mystery to embrace. Even though God will rescue us from our enemies one day, He also teaches that He wants all to be saved (see John 3:16; 1 Timothy 2:4; 2 Peter 3:9; 1 John 2:1–2). Think for a moment of the images and news of persecutions by ISIS or other threatening, hating groups. The Lord is saying that He wants the Gospel of His kingdom to reach even those sword-waving killers! Therefore, Jesus teaches us to love our enemies and pray for those who persecute us (Matthew 5:43–48). Through Christ, who suffered a martyr's death, we learn the hope that they, too, may receive God's salvation and become His children along with us.

The next time you see images of Christians bowed beneath the sword of persecution or hear stories of violence against Christians, do not fail to bow your head in prayer to the Almighty God. Ask Him to deliver His children and to deliver also the persecutors from their sin and hatred. Pray:

Deliver us in accordance with Your marvelous works and give glory to Your name, O Lord! Let all who do harm to Your servants be put to shame; let them be disgraced and deprived of all dominion and let their strength be broken. Let them know that You are the Lord, the only God, glorious over the whole world. (Song of the Three Holy Children 20–22)

We Suffer in Certain Hope

© iStockphoto.com

Even though God's people experienced periodic victory over their enemies during the time of the Maccabees, there were those among God's people who suffered greatly because they refused to compromise their faith in God. They were willing to face suffering and even death because they knew they had an eternal hope in God that could not be taken from them.

In the same way, if the day ever comes when we must face severe persecution or even death because of our faith in Christ, we can face such suffering with certain hope because we know that in Christ our many sins are completely forgiven and that we have the certain hope of the resurrection of the body and eternal life with God, who loves us.

Eleazar

One example of certain hope in the midst of suffering is found in 2 Maccabees 6:18–31, where we read about the persecution of a man by the name of Eleazar. He was being forced to eat pig's meat or else face death. He refused to eat. Some tried to convince him to obtain clean meat, which God allowed him to eat, but then pretend it was pig's meat and fool those who were watching him into thinking that he had capitulated to their request. But Eleazar responded as follows:

> *Such pretense is not worthy of our time of life, lest many of the young should suppose that Eleazar in his ninetieth year has gone over to an alien religion, and through my pretense, for the sake of living a brief moment longer, they should be led astray because of me, while I defile and disgrace my old age. For even if for the present I should avoid the punishment of men, yet whether I live or die I shall not escape the hands of the Almighty. (vv. 24–26)*

When Eleazar was later being put to death, he said:

> *It is clear to the Lord in His holy knowledge that, though I might have been saved from death, I am enduring terrible sufferings in my body under this beating, but in my soul I am glad to suffer these things because I fear Him. (v. 30)*

When Eleazar said, "I fear Him," he did not mean that he was afraid of God but that he trusted in God as his Savior (cf. Psalm 34:4, 7, 9; 130:3–4). Because of his faith in God's promises, Eleazar was able to remain faithful even unto death.

The Mother and Seven Sons

Another example of certain hope in the midst of suffering is found in 2 Maccabees 7, where we read about the persecution and death of a mother and her seven sons. They were also being forced to reject their God by eating pig's flesh or else face horrible deaths. But they refused to eat the unclean food.

A most interesting feature of this account is the comments the mother and sons share with one another. They show a deep faith in what is eternal and spiritual as well as the belief that their bodies would be restored in the resurrection. As the mother and her sons watched the first son die, they said to one another, "The Lord God is watching over us and in truth has compassion on us, as Moses declared in his song that bore witness against the people to their faces, when he said, 'And He will have compassion on His servants'" (v. 6). When the third son was about to die, he said the following about his body parts that were about to be cut off by his persecutors: "I got these from heaven, and because of His laws I disdain them, and from Him I hope to get them back again" (v. 11). In the same way, the fourth son, near death, said the following: "One cannot but choose to die at the hands of men and to cherish the hope that God gives of being raised again by Him" (v. 14). When the last son was about to die, his mother said to him, "Do not fear this butcher, but prove worthy of your brothers. Accept death, so that in God's mercy I may get you back again along with your brothers" (v. 29). The reason they had such courage and hope in the face of death was not because of any strength or character of their own, but because of their faith in God and His unfailing promises to them.

Certain Hope for Today

Christians in the Western Hemisphere have experienced years of peace and freedom when it comes to living out their faith in God. However, in other parts of the world today, fellow Christians face suffering and death because of their faith in Jesus. They can face such trials in certain hope because they know they have the victory in Jesus.

Although we may not face the kind of persecution that the Maccabees faced, our enemy is just as deadly. One of the most profound moments in our lives as believers is when we stand graveside and hear the pastor say,

> *We now commit the body . . . to the ground; earth to earth, ashes to ashes, dust to dust, in the sure and certain hope of the resurrection to eternal life through our Lord Jesus Christ, who will change our lowly bodies so that they will be like His glorious body, by the power that enables Him to subdue all things to Himself.* (Lutheran Service Book: Pastoral Care Companion *[St. Louis: Concordia Publishing House, 2007], 134.)*

Why Some Laws and Not Others?

The huge debate in modern culture, and even in some Christian churches, regarding the issue of same-sex behavior has introduced profound changes. Those who agree with God's Word that same-sex behavior is condemned along with all forms of heterosexual sins will often quote the following from Leviticus 18:22: "You shall not lie with a male as with a woman; it is an abomination" (see also Matthew 19:1–12; Romans 1:26–32; 1 Corinthians 6:9–11). However, some suggest that Christians are not being consistent when they quote Leviticus 18:22 to show that same-sex behavior is sinful. They will point out that Leviticus also condemns the eating of shrimp (Leviticus 11:9–12) and requires observance of the Sabbath Day (Leviticus 19:3, 30)—and most Christians who believe that homosexual behavior is sinful do not submit to these Old Testament laws. So, why do most Christians obey some laws of the Old Testament but ignore others?

In 1 and 2 Maccabees, we see a description of Jewish believers suffering profoundly for obeying the Old Testament laws. This article will explain why we can admire the faithfulness of these believers during the days of the Maccabees when they refused to compromise God's Word by eating "unclean foods" or profaning the Sabbath Day. It will also explain why Christians today can eat shrimp and work on Saturday—not because we despise God's Word, but because we see how these Old Testament laws have been fulfilled in Christ.

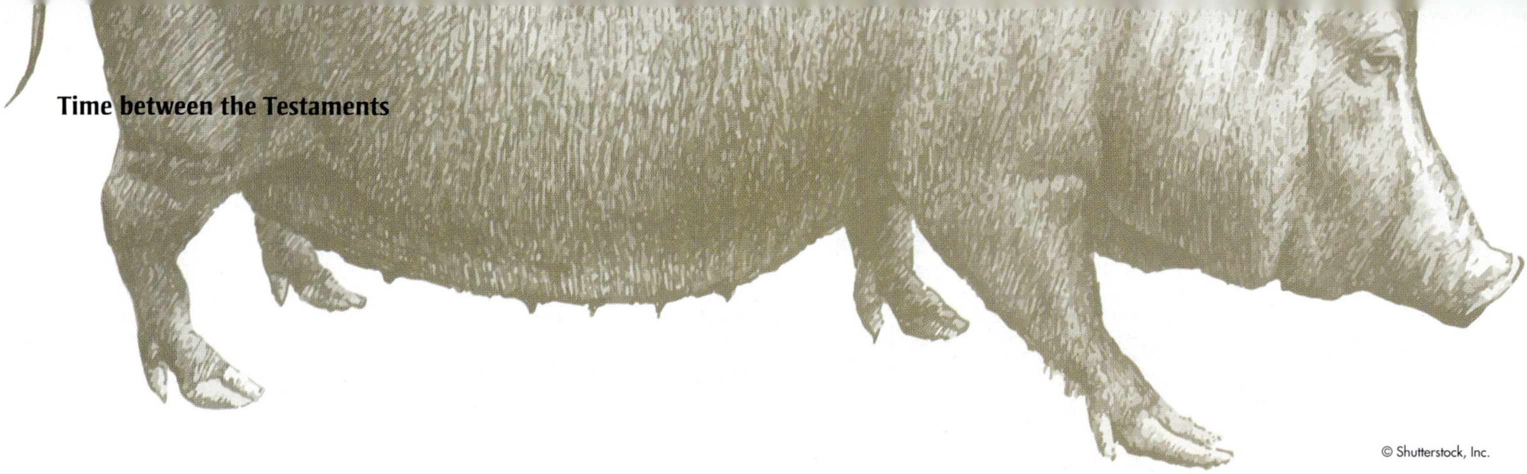

Old Testament Laws

What we must understand is that not all laws found in Leviticus or the rest of the Old Testament are of the same kind. For example, the food laws found in Leviticus 11 were given only to the people of Israel and only for a temporary period of history. The New Testament teaches that these food laws were abolished once Jesus completed His work; see Mark 7:19; Acts 10:9–16; 1 Timothy 4:1–5.

The reason God gave Old Testament Israel these food laws was to make them stand out as a unique nation through which the Savior of all nations would come into the world (Genesis 12:1–3; Romans 9:1–5). In contrast, God never commanded the Gentile nations that they could not eat shrimp or other foods that were forbidden for the people of Israel. In the same way, the Sabbath Day observance was given only to the people of Israel and this, too, was set aside when Jesus completed His work because the Sabbath ritual was a picture of the rest that we have in Christ; see Luke 6:1–11; Romans 14:5–9; Colossians 2:16–17; Hebrews 4:1–16. However, other laws were given to *all* people of *all* times and *all* places. These are God's moral laws, such as the laws of sexual prohibitions found in Leviticus 18 as well as other universal moral laws (e.g., laws against idolatry, disobeying parents, murder, theft, slander, and coveting).

THREE TYPES OF LAW

TYPE OF LAW:	Moral Law	Ceremonial Law	Civil Law
EXAMPLE:	The Ten Commandments (Exodus 20:1–17; Deuteronomy 5:6–21)	Festivals like Passover (Exodus 12)	Cutting trees down (Deuteronomy 20:19)
CHANGES:	The moral law stayed the same. Jesus and the apostles continued to teach the same moral law in the New Testament.	Jesus transformed Passover into the Lord's Supper (Matthew 26:26–29; 1 Corinthians 11:23–26).	The civil laws in the Books of Moses were especially for Israel when they settled the Promised Land. In the New Testament, the Lord teaches us to obey the just laws of the nation where we live (Romans 13:1–7).

The Maccabees's Faithfulness

Even though the food laws and the Sabbath Day observance were eventually abolished for Israel because those laws were fulfilled in Christ, during the Old Testament period before the coming of Christ, God still expected His people to obey these laws. In fact, in 1 Maccabees 1:41–64, we learn how the pagan king Antiochus Epiphanes (see 1 Maccabees 1:10) required the Jews to refrain from keeping the laws of God—and this included the expectation that the Jews were to eat "unclean foods" and work on the Sabbath Day. Many Jews refused to compromise their faith and were willing to suffer persecution and even death rather than eat "unclean foods" or work on the Sabbath Day. In doing so, they were being faithful to God, who expected them to obey His laws. We find the same concern for profaning the Sabbath in Nehemiah 13:15–18.

Jesus and the Sabbath

With this in mind, we can understand why many Jews in Jesus' day were confused and also offended when Jesus apparently allowed His own disciples to profane the Sabbath Day. In Luke 6:1–11, we read how Jesus allowed His disciples to do what some viewed as being "unlawful" on the Sabbath Day. On another Sabbath Day, Jesus performed "work" by healing the hand of a man. Many Jews wrongly concluded that Jesus was profaning the Sabbath by doing this.

Now, in one sense, the Jews of Jesus' day had reason to be concerned. One should never arrogantly rebel against God's will and disobey His laws. However, what the Jews of Jesus' day failed to understand is what Jesus said about Himself when He declared that He is "lord of the Sabbath." He claimed thereby to be God in human flesh, who could command His disciples to work on the Sabbath if He wished. Jesus even gave an example of how God allowed David to eat the bread of the Presence, which only the priests were supposed to eat. In addition, the Jews of Jesus' day failed to see that the Sabbath Day observance was not an end in itself but a picture of Christ and His work for us. In fact, their failure to see the connection between the Sabbath Day and Jesus is one of the things that kept them from believing in Jesus as their God and Savior.

So, on the one hand, during the days of Nehemiah and the Maccabees, the Jews were right to refuse to compromise God's Word by eating "unclean foods" and profaning the Sabbath Day. However, once the Messiah had come—the One to whom the food laws and the Sabbath Day observance pointed—they were to trust in Him and obey whatever He said, even if what He taught was something "new" compared to what they had known up to that point (see Luke 5:33–39). We see this important distinction in a fifth-century Christian tradition that Jesus added to His words in Luke 6:5

(a variant reading in Codex Bezae), which reads:

On the same day Jesus saw a man doing work on the Sabbath Day and said to him, "Man, if you know what you are doing, you are blessed; but if you do not know, you are cursed and a breaker of the law."

Even though scholars agree that this late, variant reading is not part of Luke's Gospel, it makes a very important point about understanding God's Law! Simply put, if Jews like Jesus' disciples were doing work on the Sabbath because they trusted the teaching of Jesus and saw Him as the reality to which the Sabbath ritual pointed, then they were blessed. However, if Jews decided to eat "unclean foods" or work on the Sabbath Day because they didn't take God or His Word seriously, then they were guilty of great sin.

Law and Gospel Opportunities

Paul writes in Colossians 2:16–17:

Therefore let no one pass judgment on you in questions of food and drink, or with regard to a festival or a new moon or a Sabbath. These are a shadow of the things to come, but the substance belongs to Christ.

Believers today should keep God's moral law and prepare themselves to answer questions from those who do not understand the changes from the Old Testament to the

New Testament. When someone questions your views on moral issues, be sure to tell that person not only the truth about God's Law but—most important—the truth about our Savior. He fulfilled the Law on our behalf, He takes away our sins, and He gives us His Holy Spirit so that we may now share in His holiness, righteousness, purity, and love for all.

God's Promises and Faith

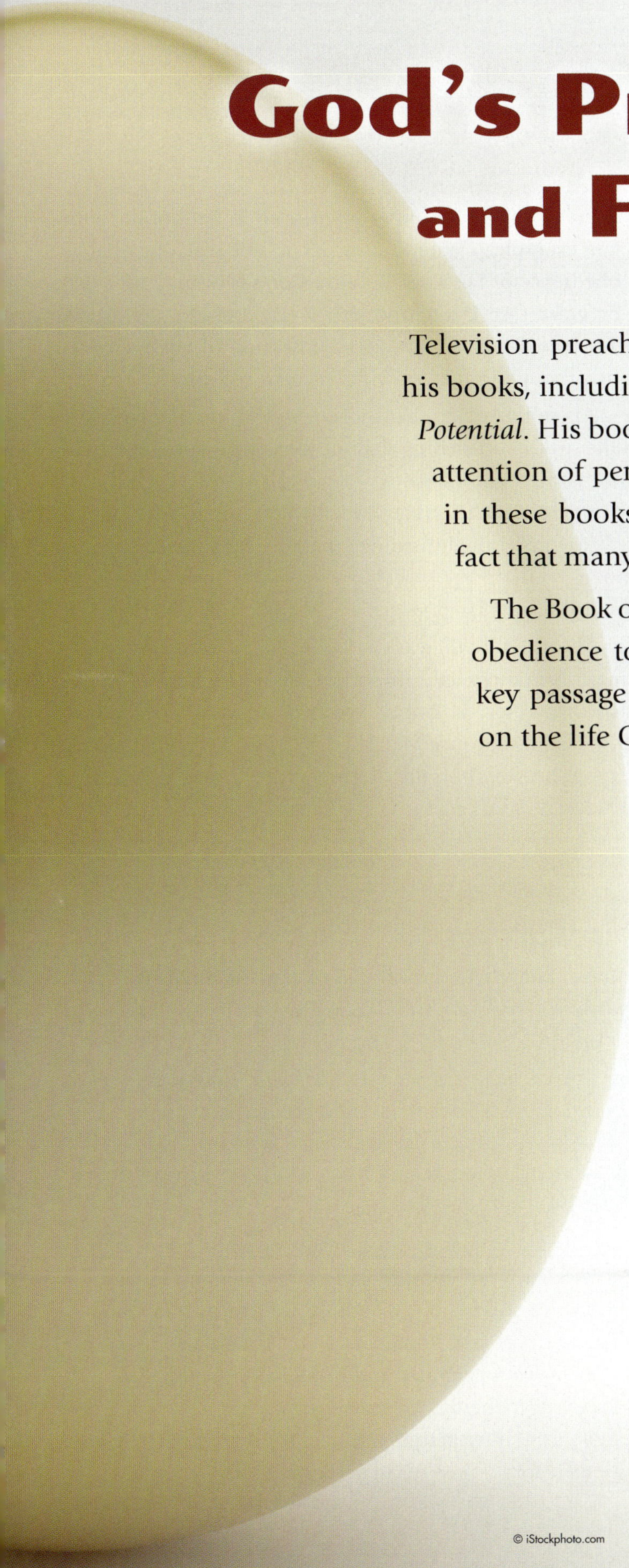

© iStockphoto.com

Television preacher Joel Osteen has gained a wide audience for his books, including *Your Best Life Now: 7 Steps to Living at Your Full Potential*. His books have sold millions of copies and garnered the attention of personalities such as Oprah. However, the teaching in these books has also raised profound questions about the fact that many believers do not experience their "best life" now.

The Book of Judith raises similar questions about prosperity, obedience to God, and suffering. This article will explore a key passage from Judith as well as New Testament passages on the life God gives us as believers.

Achior's Report

In Judith 5:5–21, we find the report of Achior, giving information about the people of Israel to Holofernes, the general of the Assyrian army. In Judith 5:17–18, Achior says the following about Israel:

As long as they did not sin against their God they prospered, for the God who hates iniquity is with them. But when they departed from the way that He had appointed for them, they were utterly defeated in very many battles and were led away captive to a foreign country; the temple of their God was razed to the ground, and their cities were captured by their enemies.

Many Jews in Jesus' day may have been thinking of this section of Judith when they were hoping that Jesus would conquer the Romans and give God's people earthly peace and prosperity. Certainly, there are sections of the Old Testament that teach that as long as we refrain from sin and live holy lives God will bless us with earthly protection, peace, and prosperity. For example, in Deuteronomy 28, we read about blessings that God's people could expect if they obeyed God's laws versus curses that they could expect if they disobeyed God's laws.

Deuteronomy 28 Explained

However, this teaching of Deuteronomy 28 must be interpreted in light of the entire message of Holy Scripture. For example, Deuteronomy 28 is not teaching that we merit God's blessings by our obedience of His laws, because God's blessings are always undeserved and given to us by grace (see Deuteronomy 7:7–11; 8:11–20; 9:1–6). We obey God because of His mercy (see Romans 2:4; 12:1–2). Because of His mercy, He chooses to reward our obedience, though imperfect, with His many blessings.

In addition, Deuteronomy 28 is not teaching that those who live in repentance and faith will never suffer in this life; nor is it teaching that all those who suffer are being punished for their disobedience and rebellion against God. For example, even though Job was a "righteous man" (i.e., a repentant believer), God allowed Him to suffer greatly for reasons of His own. But Job's friends wrongly assumed that Job was suffering because of some secret, unrepentant sin.

We find the same mystery expressed in Psalm 73, where Asaph wonders why unbelievers experience peace and prosperity, whereas God's faithful people suffer greatly. Asaph confesses that pondering this mystery led him to have sinful thoughts that God was not being faithful or trustworthy (see vv. 2–16). We find the same evil thinking about God among the Jews of Malachi's day (see Malachi 2:17). However, God rescued Asaph from his sinful thinking by showing him the destiny of the wicked versus those who trust in God (Psalm 73:17–28).

New Testament Perspective

Jesus said to His disciples: "I have said these things to you, that in Me you may have peace. In the world you will have tribulation. But take heart; I have overcome the world" (John 16:33). Also, Peter wrote:

> *In [salvation] you greatly rejoice, though now for a little while, if necessary, you have been grieved by various trials, so that the tested genuineness of your faith . . . may be found to result in praise and glory and honor at the revelation of Jesus Christ. . . . Rejoice insofar as you share Christ's sufferings, that you may also rejoice and be glad when His glory is revealed.* (1 Peter 1:6–7; 4:13)

Sometimes we experience suffering as a direct result of sinful choices we have made, and God uses such suffering to call us to repentance and faith in His Son. Sometimes we suffer simply because we live in a fallen creation that is in bondage to decay (see Romans 8:18–25). God also uses this kind of suffering to call us to repentance and hope in Christ. Finally, sometimes we suffer because we are being persecuted for the name of Jesus (see Matthew 5:10–12). When we suffer in this way, we must remember that we are blessed because we have forgiveness of sin and eternal hope in Jesus.

Our Best Life to Come

God never promised to give us our best life now. We certainly should not expect God to bless us because of our obedience, as though we deserve His blessings, for, in spite of our best efforts, we remain sinners who deserve nothing but God's wrath. God mercifully gives us many earthly blessings, and we strive to obey Him because of His mercy toward us in Christ. However, when God does allow believers to suffer, it is not because He has forsaken us. In fact, God promises to use trials and suffering to bless us—His forgiven children in Christ! (See Romans 5:1–5.)

No matter what life you face or enjoy today, know that your best life is the one to come. Before Jesus went to the cross, He assured His disciples that He was going to the Father to prepare a place for them (John 14:2). Later, in Revelation 7:15–17, the Lord showed the apostle John what that life to come would be like, a heavenly prosperity beyond all that we enjoy here. Therefore, lift up your head in hope and pray like the early Christians, "Our Lord, come!" (1 Corinthians 16:22).

Foolish Eyes, and Wise

The apostle Paul writes in 2 Corinthians 5:7, "We walk by faith, not by sight." Simply put, unbelievers refuse to believe what they cannot see or understand. In contrast, the Holy Spirit moves us to trust God's Word, even though at times what we see and experience in this life seems to conflict with God's promises.

We find the same teaching in Hebrews 11:1–3:

Now faith is the assurance of things hoped for, the conviction of things not seen. For by it the people of old received their commendation. By faith we understand that the universe was created by the word of God, so that what is seen was not made out of things that are visible.

The author of Hebrews speaks of "the people of old" who "received their commendation" because they lived by faith. "The people of old" were believers during the Old Testament period who lived by faith before the coming of Christ—and one of these "people of old" was the author of the Wisdom of Solomon.

A Pleasing Book

Even though Luther and many others throughout history did not include the Wisdom of Solomon as part of the Old Testament canon, Luther had the following to say about the Wisdom of Solomon in his preface to this book:

There are many good things in this book, and it is well worth reading. . . . It pleases me beyond measure that the author . . . extols the Word of God so highly, and ascribes to the Word all the wonders God has performed. . . . This book is a proper exposition and illustration of the first commandment. (AE 35:340–44)

© Aldo Murillo/iStockphoto.com

One example of godly teaching in the Wisdom of Solomon is found in 1:16–3:13, where the author explains the difference between how unbelievers view reality and how believers view reality. Unbelievers live by sinful sight:

> *For they reasoned unsoundly, saying to themselves, "Short and sorrowful is our life and there is no remedy at the death of a human being. . . . Because we were born by mere chance, and hereafter we shall be as though we had never been . . . come, therefore, let us enjoy the good things that exist and make use of the creation to the full as in youth. . . . Let none of us fail to share in our revelry, everywhere let us leave signs of enjoyment, because this is our portion and this our lot. . . . Let our might be our law of right, for what is weak proves itself to be useless. Let us lie in wait for the righteous man, because he is inconvenient to us and opposes our actions; he reproaches us for sins against the law. . . . He professes to have knowledge of God and calls himself a child of the Lord. . . . Let us see if his words are true, and let us test what will happen at the end of his life; for if the righteous man is God's son, He will help him and will deliver him from the hand of his adversaries."* (2:1, 2, 6, 9, 11–12, 13, 17–18)

© iStockphoto.com

Here we see that, like many unbelievers today, these people see human life as an accident of a meaningless universe and death as the end of human existence. They therefore wish to indulge every desire for the sake of momentary pleasure, and they despise the believer who points them to our Creator, who teaches us about creation, sin, repentance, and salvation. In fact, they persecute the believer, assuming that if God exists He will not allow one who believes in Him to suffer. Such people live by sinful human sight and refuse to trust God's Word. Of course, there are some unbelievers who strive to live virtuous lives because of the Law of God written on their hearts (see Romans 2:14–16). But their motivation for doing good things flows from their sinful nature, and so they give glory to themselves for their virtuous deeds rather than giving all glory to God.

© Gong Hangxu/iStockphoto.com

© iStockphoto.com

Living by Faith

In contrast, the author of the Wisdom of Solomon writes the following about those who live by faith:

> *But the souls of the righteous are in the hand of God, and no torment will ever touch them. In the eyes of the foolish they seemed to have died, . . . but they are at peace. For though in the sight of men they were punished, their hope is full of immortality. Having been disciplined a little, they will receive great good, because God tested them . . . and like a sacrificial whole burnt offering He accepted them. . . . Those who trust in Him will understand truth, and the faithful will abide with Him in love, because grace and mercy are upon His holy ones, and He watches over His chosen.* (3:1–6, 9)

Here we see that believers trust in God for mercy and eternal life, even though they may not comprehend God's ways and even though they face suffering and death in this life.

By faith in God's Word, we know that we are forgiven and holy in God's sight through faith in Christ, even though all we see are the many sins of thought, word, and deed we struggle with daily. By faith in God's Word, we look forward to the resurrection of the body and eternal life with God, even though suffering and death is all we see in this life. The Wisdom of Solomon teaches us the difference between living by sight and living by faith.